Cortney Grubbs

Confessing Captivity

Queer Narratives of Trauma by American Women Writers

LAP LAMBERT Academic Publishing

Impressum / Imprint
Bibliografische Information der Deutschen Nationalbibliothek: Die Deutsche Nationalbibliothek verzeichnet diese Publikation in der Deutschen Nationalbibliografie; detaillierte bibliografische Daten sind im Internet über http://dnb.d-nb.de abrufbar.

Bibliographic information published by the Deutsche Nationalbibliothek: The Deutsche Nationalbibliothek lists this publication in the Deutsche Nationalbibliografie; detailed bibliographic data are available in the Internet at http://dnb.d-nb.de.

Coverbild / Cover image: www.ingimage.com

Verlag / Publisher:
LAP LAMBERT Academic Publishing
ist ein Imprint der / is a trademark of
OmniScriptum GmbH & Co. KG
Heinrich-Böcking-Str. 6-8, 66121 Saarbrücken, Deutschland / Germany
Email: info@lap-publishing.com

Herstellung: siehe letzte Seite /
Printed at: see last page
ISBN: 978-3-659-54812-3

Zugl. / Approved by: Gainesville, University of Florida, Diss., 2010

To my beloved chosen family

Acknowledgements

This project gestated for over three years before it became a labor of love—off and on for five years. I cannot thank Marsha Bryant enough for all of her support, guidance, and fabulosity. I would like to thank my committee members: Kenneth Kidd, Jodi Schorb, and Anita Anatharam; these are truly magnificent beings, and I am fortunate that they have chosen to work with me. I also owe a debt of gratitude to Lisa Logan, Pamela Gilbert, Aaron Talbot, Joel Adams, Idoia Gorosabel-Gkikas, Erica NIckolaidis, Jennifer Simmons—and all of the graduate students, staff, and undergraduate students at the University of florida.

My parents, Roger and Debra, are responsible for preparing, encouraging, and supporting me through this endeavor; and, my sister, Meagan, has been both a protector and laughing agent when I needed her. Without my family's strength and love, I would not have been able to complete this project. Also, I would like to convey my gratitude to my partner, Donna, who believed that this project would one day be published.

Finally, I wish to thank several individuals at my current home institution, Gordon State College, who have continually been a source of support— particularly Edward Whitelock, Rhonda Wilcox, , Laura Shadrick, Steve Raynie, Caesar Perkowski, Perry Ivey, Susan Hendricks, Anna Higgins, and Doug Davis.

Table of Contents

Chapter 1: Introduction

Even before trauma became a recognized discourse, American women were writing about the experiences of living with trauma. In these writings, women did not seek to hide or negate the effects of their traumas, which oftentimes separated them from their respective communities. Rather, they confessed—and actively embraced—their queer identity as a means to foster a witnessing public. This tradition of confessional American women's writing negotiates and ultimately queers private and public spaces, literary genres, and the boundaries between popular and literary texts. One of the goals of my project is to examine how women asserted their experiences and identities while resisting erasure based on their sex and trauma. As early as Mary Rowlandson, women of the Americas were engaging with the masculine tradition of confessional writing, primarily originating with St. Augustine's autobiographical work *Confessions*. Women of the early republic continued to re-imagine confessionalism as a queer space for articulating agency and trauma as they became popular novelists. While many male and female readers flocked to read the texts in hopes of becoming privy to scandalous confessions, the texts operate in such a way that reconstructs the act and purpose of confession. Building off the work of Michel Foucault, Judith Herman, and Ann Cvetkovich, this project contributes to discussions of confessionalism, counter-publics, and trauma in dialogue with each other while exploring how American women's writing queers each one of those discourses. Mary Rowlandson's captivity narrative and Hannah Foster's novel *The Coquette* will serve as the originating points for this tradition of American women's confessional writing, which continues even today. Though I will not be able to discuss every American woman's confessional text, I hope to provide a portrait of the span of the tradition.

6

In my project, my task is to acknowledge a tradition of American women's confessional writing that queers binaries of gender and sex. This tradition transforms the landscape of domesticity into a public and political space by confessing trauma; in recognizing the existence of violence within domesticity, along with the act of confessing it, these writers dissolve the invisible the separation between public and private spaces. This separation between public and private spaces is related to the construction of gender and sex—and also the categoricalizaiton of literary/popular and logic/emotive. Originating with Mary Rowlandson's captivity narrative and continuing to evolve with Hannah Webster Foster's seduction novel, this tradition of American women's confessional writing revolutionizes the traditional way that we—as critics, teachers, and historians—have viewed early American women's writing, the nature of trauma, and the act of confession.

Rowlandson recognizes—and embraces—the performative nature of confession and uses it as a platform to create a counter-public. The purpose of this counter-public is to validate agency of trauma survivors while witnessing trauma. In order to preserve her identity while articulating "the unspeakable", Rowlandson marks her inability to fully explain her experiences by inserting biblical passages; these passages, referring to the trials and miraculous triumphs, juxtapose Rowlandson's very concrete and ambivalent feelings regarding her captivity and captors. Thus, captivity becomes a method in which to articulate trauma. In the late 18th century, Hannah Webster Foster's *The Coquette* evokes the captivity narrative and continues the tradition that Rowlandson began. Foster's novel, based on a true story, centers around a woman who suffers trauma because of the normalization of gender, class, and domesticity. Ostracized by her "friends" in higher classes who abide by gender expectations, the chief protagonist becomes a matron and is literally forced into the schemes of a rapist. Moreover, the rapes occur in the protagonist's mother's home—solidifying the fact that domestic spaces are political and potentially violent. *The Coquette* also revises the way in which silence operates within the act of confession—and makes a firm distinction between being silenced and choosing silence as a method of articulating trauma.

Contemporary Expectations of Confession

Confessionalism is often discussed as a modern, pop-culture phenomenon that is regulated to poetry and television talk-shows; the 1950s and onward are considered the pinnacle points for the genre of confessional writing. Discussions of women's confessional writing typically gravitate toward a vexed mixture of feminism and sensationalism. Elizabeth Wilson writes, "Women seized on the confessional genre as a way of giving consciousness-raising a more permanent form. In this writing, women expressed their 'radical otherness' and 'made strange' the familiar world by reason of their angle of vision" (28). The term "confessional poetry" was coined in the 1950s to describe Robert Lowell's book of poetry; and it was subsequently applied to both male and female poets—such as his students, Sexton and Plath. Yet, as Elizabeth Gregory argues in "Confessing the Body", as women gained visibility within confessional poetry, confessionalism was gendered 'private' and 'trivial': "Though the mode first appeared in the work of male poets, it is often associated with its female practitioners, and condemned as trivial and self-indulgent" (33). The general assumptions surrounding the content of women's confessionalism is also important to note. Topics such as mental illness and sexual desire are certainly the popularized themes of women's confessionalism. The continuation of such cultural expectations has validated texts that share those common themes of mental distress and sexuality, such as Susanna Kaysen's *Girl,*

8

Interrupted and Elizabeth Wurtzel's *Prozac Nation*. While Kaysen's and Wurtzel's texts are certainly valuable, they nonetheless demonstrate the willingness to label some texts 'confessional' over others. In *Remembered Rapture*, bell hooks discusses how the conflation of both 'women's confessional writing' and mental illness undermines the literary merit of the texts: "However, writing is not therapy. Unlike therapy, where anything may be spoken in any manner, the very notion of craft suggests that the writer must necessarily edit, shape, and play with words in a manner that is always subordinated to desired intent and effect" (14). Recognizing the literary craft involved in writing is one method of recognizing the significance of women's confessional writing.

When women's confessional writing is acknowledged— like in cases like Sylvia Plath and Anne Sexton—even critics seem unable to untangle the author's biography and literary prowess, sometimes inadvertently creating spectacles out of both the author and work. My examples of Plath and Sexton are not haphazard; rather, I chose them because of the implicit assumption that women's confessional literature as relegated to the form of poetry. Yet, I find it odd that very few teachers or critics deem Anne Bradstreet a confessional poet—even though she certainly is and wrote about her fears of childbirth and even the fear of her critics devaluing her work as a publishing woman in the 16th-Century. What is gained when reading Bradstreet as confessional? Certainly, the expectations and functions of confession are expanded; and, I would argue that Bradstreet's act of traversing across public and private boundaries is more evident. And, as a teacher, I would argue that acknowledging the confessionalism in Bradstreet's work offers the possibilities of discussing her literary prowess and the experiences within her poems that many women undoubtedly experienced (and continue to experience)—along with the specific traumas that she experienced, such as surviving her children and losing her home to a fire. Also, the potential exists to place her in dialogue with other women's confessional writing, such as Plath—who discusses ambivalency surrounding motherhood; doing so is both exciting and radical for both students and teachers because it allows us to really examine cultural and political changes and stagnations as they relate to women.

If women's confessional culture is thought to be one other place, it would be the television. Mass-circulated as the subject of talk shows, women's confessionalism is popularized by celebrities such as Oprah Winfrey, Sally Jessie Raphael, and Riki Lake. While Winfrey has revamped her stage and physically distanced herself from her audience since the 1980s, assuming the more highbrow-end of the spectrum, the subject of women's confessionalism is largely considered a lowbrow form of entertainment *for* women. These types of talk shows are also snubbed, called "Trash TV". Although I think that television provides a legitimate avenue to create a counter-public, there is an entire tradition of American women's confessional writing that is generally being ignored. In fact, I believe that this tradition of writing is actually responsible for the development of 'talk-TV.'

Expanding the Confessional Model

My goal is to examine a tradition of American women's confessional writing that begins with Mary Rowlandson's 17th-Century *The Captivity and Restoration of Mrs. Mary Rowlandson* and Hannah Foster's 18th-Century seduction novel *The Coquette*. This tradition's goal is not to confess guilt, but to articulate trauma and create a woman-centric counter-public; I believe that this distinct tradition of confessionalism is neither fully cultivated in nor reactionary to the Foucauldian model. Michel Foucault's historical analysis of confession in his first volume of

10

The History of Sexuality is largely accepted as the prominent discussion on the topic of confession. Foucault's theories rely on a European and masculine tradition of the confessional writing that originates with the writings of St. Augustine and Jean-Jacques Rousseau. As Foucault discusses, this Eurocentric masculine tradition of confessionalism privileges particular themes, goals, and voices. In Foucault's binary model of confession, there are two individuals: the confessor (the person who confesses) and confessant (the person who hears the confession). Typically, sexual desires provide the content of confessions; and the ritual of confession supposedly liberates the confessor by uncovering truth. However, the same dynamics that construct knowledge and power govern confession: "it is also a ritual that unfolds within a power relationship, for one does not confess without the presence (or virtual presence) of a partner who is not simply the interlocutor but the authority who requires the confession, prescribes and appreciates it and intervenes in order to judge, punish, forgive, console, and reconcile" (Foucault 61-2). This "scheme for transforming sex into discourse" (Foucault 20) provided a succinct and effective method to create, maintain, and police subjectivities. Foucault argues that "the obligation to confess is now relayed through so many different points, is so deeply ingrained in us, that we no longer perceive it as the effect of a power that constrains us" (60); rather, we have become caught up in the ruse of this "regulated and polymorphous incitement to discourse" (Foucault 34). Foucault offers his final verdict: "Western man has become a confessing animal" (59).

A couple of theorists, notably Judith Butler and Peter Brooks, have offered alternative interpretations of the Foucauldian confessional model in order to validate the agency of the confessor. In *Undoing Gender*, Judith Butler revises the popularized Foucauldian confessee-confessor model to include a third dimension: the bodily act of articulation. This speech act, Butler argues, is not the material desire or deed committed; rather, the act of speaking is *another* bodily deed and reveals the performative nature of confessionalism. And, in *Troubling Confessions*, lawyer and literary critic Peter Brooks continues Butler's revision of the Foucauldian confessional model; he suggests that the act of confession imposes guilt—which means that regardless of the *content* of the confession, guilt is created by the *act* of confessing. In this manner, Brooks is trying to transfer the guilt from the content of the confession—for example, queer identities or desires—onto the actual act of confession itself. But even within the Butler's and Brooks' revision of the confessional model, the confessor is still portrayed as unable to fully achieve subjectivity; and the act of confession continues to exist as a technology of both power and knowledge that is maintained by the confessant.

Like both Butler and Brooks, I will present a revision of Foucault's confessional model; but I will also support my revision with writings not explored by Foucault. I postulate that confession is not comprised of two participants, but *three*. My triangular model includes the positionality of 'witness.' This position of "witness" includes those listening or reading the confession, as well as the confessor at some points—and even the confessant, if s/he chooses to willingly abnegate authority. My model is striking because no one, under any circumstances, absorbs power from the confessor. Though, witnesses do hold the power to transfer the confessor's power and agency that the confessant attempts to otherwise appropriate. I believe the power of witnessing, this third dimension of the confessional model, is apparent even in the history and that Foucault bases his theories upon. For instance, Foucault sites the history of the Catholic confessionalism as existing between the supposed sinner and the priest; yet, what about the 'witnesses': deities? In the Anglican faith, of course, confession occurs amidst the congregation—rendering the witnesses visible. The existence of witnesses is powerful because it complicates the power structure of both the act of confession and the confessional model. While the witness may exist in the masculine tradition of confession, it is most visible—and active—in the tradition of women's confessional writing that I explore. Moreover, I am not arguing that this tradition of women's confessional writing originated in opposition to the masculine tradition of confession. Rather, I believe that this tradition arose in response to articulating women's experiences of trauma and creating a space, a counter-public, where they could be heard.

Counter-publics

In this project, I argue that American women's confessional writing fosters a counter-public—complete with a space, a community, and a discourse—in order fulfill a need: to find a method for articulating pain that was socially ignored. In *Publics and Counterpublics*, Michael Warner expands the Hambermassian theory on publics and explains that counter-publics are defined "by their conflict with the norms and contexts of their cultural environment" (63):

> some publics are defined by their tension with a larger public. Their participants are marked off from persons or citizens in general. Discussions within such a public is understood to contravene the rules obtaining in the world at large, being structured by alternative dispositions or protocols, making different assumptions about what can be said or what goes without saying. This kind of public is, in effect, a counterpublic: it maintains at some level, conscious or not, an awareness of its subordinate status. (56)

Warner cites examples, such as gay and women's cultures, as being counter-publics. This subversive space is historically acknowledged in the feminist conscious-raising groups of the 1960s where women gathered in order to tell the truths of their lives and create public awareness about issues affecting women. While I believe that this desire to promote social change resurged in the 1960s, ironically on the heels of confessional poetry's acknowledged emergence, this was not the first time that such a space or public was created. I believe that counter-publics were created long before they are acknowledged. This project concentrates on the qualities and tradition of American women's confessional counter-publics, but I am confident that these counter-publics—both sharing and deviating from the ones discussed here—can be found in other traditions, cultures, and countries.

Clearly, counter-publics can be powerful; and precisely because of that fact, often they are seen as a viable threat to hegemony. And, I will argue that this is why American women's confessional writing is a tradition that has been largely ignored, censored and restricted. One method by which this tradition has been contained is by the expectations, discussed earlier, placed upon women's confessional writing; labeled as private, and therefore trivial, the tradition has been dismissed as socially unimportant and literarily insignificant. But, these expectations can adequately summarize colonial and modern perceptions of women's writing—why is that? I am certain that the fear surrounding the publication of materials written by women is firmly founded on the anxiety that a counter-public would, indeed, strengthen if visible and acknowledged. The purpose of a counter-public is to create a community and public discourse that deviates from the homogeneous group; so, it would stand to reason that this homogeneous group would not want to acknowledge—which is in itself a form of validation—the existence of counter-publics. I believe that this resistance to acknowledging counter-publics is not only present in historical discourse, but literary discourse as well. Literary history and the canon have been dominated by men, which is evident by the celebration of F.O. Matthissen's *American*

Renaissance.[1] Actively beginning in the 1980s, feminist critics, such as Jane Tompkins, strove to "open up the canon" and recognize the literary and social consequence of early American women's contributions.[2] This quest to rediscover texts by women continues today.

In 2009, Elaine Showalter published a project that is one of the *first* of its kind: a literary history of American women's writing. In *A Jury of Her Peers: American Women Writers from Anne Bradstreet to Annie Proulx*, Showalter takes on the monumental task of "tell[ing] the story of American women's writing with a beginning, middle, and end" (xv). She argues that this particular tradition originates from social and literary circumstances, versus biological ones: "the female tradition in American literature is not the result of biology, anatomy, or psychology. It comes from women's relation to the literary marketplace and from literary influence rather than essential sexual difference" (xv). This project, like Showalter's, does not argue that traditions of American women's writing are essentialist, neither in relation to the author or the audience who can relate to the texts; this project, however, focuses on a distinct tradition within American women's writing: confessionalism. American women's confessional writing, I argue, does not originate solely "from women's relation to the literary marketplace" (Showalter xv)—though I agree with Showalter that American women's literature, in general, emerges with political and public aims. Rather, I will argue that the American women's confessional writing emerges as a method to create a counter-public, whose focus is to validate agency and witness confessions of trauma. Like Showalter's project, tracing the herstory of American women's confessional writing is an ambitious one. Not only does the tradition span over several centuries, but it also challenges views of confessionalism, trauma, genre and virtually every general category—from constructions of gender and sex to adult and young adult or child. Showalter admits to having made "selections, distinctions, and judgments" (xv) in her project; but what I find intriguing that she discusses only two out of the six texts, written by women, that appear in my project. I believe that these confessional texts, and possibly the tradition as a whole, exist within the gaps of 'literary history'—even within accounts of women's literary history.

The Discourse of Trauma

Trauma is an experience, but it is also a discourse. As Anne Cvetkovich argues in *An Archive of Feelings*, trauma is more than a diagnosis—it is a historical discourse, a modern method of legitimating psychic wounds that may not be visible. She notes that beginning in the 19th-Century, "the term *trauma*, which had previously referred to a physical would, came to be applied to mental or physical distress" (Cvetkovich 17). Extreme trauma is generally used to describe survivors of historically recognized instances of war and genocide, notably the Holocaust; and it is most often discussed in terms of physical—and visible—wounds. In 1980, Post-Traumatic Stress Disorder (PTSD) became more publically visible when it appeared in the American Psychiatric Association's diagnostic manual; the diagnosis was chiefly used in relation to Vietnam veterans, who were mostly men. In the late 1980s, a few small-scale studies were conducted to prove that there was a high rate of PTSD-symptoms among female survivors of domestic violence, sexual assault, and incest.[3] In the 1990s, psychiatrist Judith Herman helped to revolutionize the ways in which trauma is conceptualized with the publication of *Trauma and Recovery*. Notably, the text explicitly shows how political, legal, and economic inequality against women is connected to domestic and sexual violence against women. This ground-breaking text explores the psychological conditions of battered women, comparing them to domestic captives and prisoners of war; moreover,

Herman does not shirk away from discussing the taboo subject of rape as an act of violence, versus a sexual act, between married spouses. Cvetkovich deviates from Herman's work, in several ways, including focusing on a public that is not really acknowledged in Herman's work: the queer (particularly lesbian) public. Cvetkovich succinctly places Herman's theories on trauma and Judith Butler's theories on gender in dialogue with each other: "Even though [Judith] Butler doesn't name it as such, the normalization of sex and gender identities can be seen as a form of insidious trauma, which is effective precisely because it often leaves no sign of a problem" (46). Significantly, Betty Friedman—the author of the celebrated feminist text *The Female Mystique* in 1963—dubbed the inequality of women the "problem without a name" (qtd. in Herman 28), which reiterates the insidious nature of violence resulting from constructions of gender and sex. Although I cannot argue that their gender and sex are the sole reasons that these female authors—or their protagonists— experience trauma; as this project will explore, the constructions of gender and sex overlap and fuse with other constructions—such as race, class, sexuality, and even mental illness.

Within the tradition of American women's confessional writing that I am exploring, witnessing confessions of trauma are the focus—even before the discourses of trauma, as we currently know it, originated. Clearly, words such as "trauma" and "gender" did not mean the same to Mary Rowlandson as they do to contemporaneous readers. But, to argue that women in the past did not have the mental faculties or experiences to comprehend cultural expectations of gender or the emotional responses to atrocities is to do a great disservice to both the individuals and their texts—and their readers. I do not feel like I am inscribing my interpretations upon these texts; rather, I think that there is enough evidence that any reasonable reader would agree that these women did suffer with traumatic symptoms—and that they braved social and moral ridicule in order to articulate their experiences. I am more interested in seeing *what the texts can teach us* about trauma, witnessing, and the creation of counter-publics. For the purposes of this project, "trauma" is not defined as a social wound or a medical diagnosis that can be cured or erased. No, this project's purpose is to aid in the quest of finding ways to articulate that which is unspeakable and what is often forgotten. The narrative voices of the texts that I engage do encounter acts of physical violence—torture, rape, and medical captivity; but they do not seek to privilege or create a hierarchy of trauma. Rather, these narrative voices collectively strive to create a narrative structure that reveals the profound physical and psychic effects of trauma—and how an individual can resist erasure and retain her agency.

Although trauma theory continues to evolve, one theme has remained persistent since Freud: loss—the loss of feelings (disassociation with others and one's self), memory (amnesia), and even identity (sense of self). These internal struggles sometimes result in external losses—the loss of relationships, employment, and even the inability to find joy in life. Indeed, these losses combine to form something akin to a large, gaping hole. It is no coincidence that *trauma* originated in the nineteenth century to describe a physical, visual wound; and even though trauma now refers to psychic, as well as physical, pain, it is still marked with an overarching premise of loss. One of the goals of this project is to reclaim one particular loss and queer it: the loss of identity. As a result of this presumed loss of identity, confession is seen as prominent avenue for healing that must take place in order to fill this void. Instead of emphasizing the gaps or wounds in identity, this project concentrates on the creation of queer identities and counter-publics by trauma survivors. Cvetkovich explores "the cultural memory of trauma as central to the formation of identities and publics"

18

(38) as it relates to a performative archive of lesbian experiences; this project similarly analyzes a woman's archive, but also spans over a lengthier time and concentrates on confessional writing. But like Cvetkovich, and unlike Herman, this project does not privilege the domestic sphere as the space where violence against women is most predominant. Rather, this project analyzes how trauma and captivity transcend—and finally queer—the public and private spheres.

Most theorists agree that a traumatic experience is one that involves violence and a sense of danger; Herman defines trauma as an experience that:

> overwhelm[s] the ordinary human adaptations to life. Unlike commonplace misfortunes, traumatic events generally involve threats to life or bodily integrity, or a close personal encounter with violence and death. They confront human beings with the extremities of helplessness and terror, and evoke the responses of catastrophe. (33)

Like Cvetkovich's work, this project focuses on the affective responses toward trauma—the feelings of "helplessness and terror" (Herman 33) that arise from threats of violence, which are not necessarily directed at the material body. Most psychiatrists would agree that traumatic events[4] create an excess of external stimuli that overloads the brain; unable to "process" or compartmentalize the event, the brain responds with varying combinations of hyperarousal, disassociation, and numbness. Especially in the 1980s and 1990s when more women's stories of rape and incest began to be shared publically, "disassociation" was commonly thought to be the standard reaction and Multiple Personality Disorder[5] was often diagnosed in these women. Although the "split" of personalities is not as routinely assumed in survivors of rape and incest as it was, the same basic rhetoric that someone is "not whole"—or "broken"—is still pervasive. Herman gives great credit to survivors of trauma when she asserts that their mind and affective responses are going into

19

overdrive even as they seem to be immobile and unaffected; however, she ultimately asses that "Psychological trauma is an affliction of the powerless" (33). One primary aim of my project is to reclaim the space of trauma and the agency of survivors as queer—and at no time envision survivors as damaged or broken, even if they feel as if they are. In other words, this allows a survivor to *feel* helpless while remaining whole—though feeling wholly terrified. In this project, I refuse to engage in the rhetoric of powerlessness, even when survivors are rendered physically immobile or psychologically and emotively stunned.

Any discussion of trauma, especially one that involves archival, is going to face the difficult task of locating—and then finding ways to speak about—trauma. This is not to say that instances of trauma are uncommon; but, rather, trauma is connected to the abuse of power—and anyone who has tried to speak about power (and not only its effects) knows the problems therein. (Recognizing trauma, though, is something comparable to identifying gender—we 'normally' know it when we see it. But that's not really the case, either; because unless we are looking for trauma, it may (more often than not) escape our attention. Three situations attribute to this: the access granted to trauma is based on one's access to power (race, class, gender, etc. play a vital role); trauma eludes, if not destroys, language; and individual, as well as cultural, memory of trauma is very difficult to maintain. The first instance has been alluded to already when discussing the historical discourse of trauma. In this way, discussions about trauma are inherently queer because they attempt to speak about the *unspeakable*. In *The Body in Pain*, Elaine Scarry explains that pain is not only difficult to articulate—but it defies traditional forms of communication: "Physical pain does not simply resist language but actively destroys it" (4). Because trauma puts pressure on language, it also requires alternative forms of recognition and archiving; Ann Cvetkovich writes about the struggles surrounding archival:

> Because trauma can be unspeakable and unrepresentable and because it is marked by forgetting and disassociation, it often seems to leave behind no records at all. Trauma puts pressure on conventional forms of documentation, representation, and commemoration, giving rise to new genres of expression, such as testimony, and new forms of monuments, rituals, and performances that can call into being collective witnesses and publics. (7)

Archives are vital in many areas, such as gay history and experiences and trauma. When experiences and identities are actively ignored and invalidated, archival efforts are both difficult as well as vital. One of the major hurdles that archivalists, psychologists, and theorists face is the resistance of memory to trauma. Judith Herman writes, "The ordinary response to atrocities is to banish them from consciousness" (1). In order to preserve a cohesive, normalized sense of self, a survivor chooses or is forced to vanquish the feelings and experiences that disrupt this normalized sense of self.

Captivity

I believe that one way that American women's confessional writing creates a visible archive is by evoking the captivity narrative. Within our cultural imagination, *captivity* evokes images of war, torture, and individuals being torn away from their homes. These violent images are accompanied with being physically caged or imprisoned, outside of one's familiar environment. Mostly, the word 'captivity' is associated with animals, mainly in zoos, and to stories that have long since found themselves either mythologized in history or literary anthologies. 'Captivity' has been regulated, especially in the American cultural imagination, to political prisoners or history—either way, something far-off and not immediate to one's common experiences. To *live within captivity* seems impossible for us to envision, so much so that we spend lavish amounts of money and time on creating a façade of entertainment and education surrounding zoos, along with public safety and rehabilitation with regard to prisons and jails.

An example would be the misappropriation of power—or, more accurately, torture—at Guantanamo Bay; there, many women, children, and elderly people were tortured and killed even after they were proven to have no knowledge or involvement with terrorist plots against the United States.[6] The government had no logical reason to confine, much less to defy the Geneva Code by torturing these individuals; as Anne McClintock brilliantly argues, the visual images and knowledge of the captives reinforced the belief that the United States was retaliating against a visible, material enemy. Popular images of captivity vacillate between being overtly politics and romantic fantasy. How many times do we, as audience members, end up rooting for the captors—or even for the captive and captor to fall in love—in films? Think about Hannibal Lector, a much beloved serial killer protagonist, whom we want to fall in love with a pretty FBI detective—or 'Beauty' from the fable *Beauty and the Beast*. These romantic and sentimental notions may be helpful in creating cultural amnesia regarding the traumatic effects of captivity.

Perhaps it is no coincidence that 'the Beast'[7] becomes human after he begs for forgiveness and acquires Beauty's love. Herman acknowledges, "Attachment between hostage and captor is the rule rather than the exception. Prolonged confinement while in fear of death and in isolation from the outside world reliably produces a bond of identification between captor and victim" (82). This "attachment" has been labeled "Stockholm syndrome." The diagnosis was coined after hostages who were held for 131 hours at gun-point in a Swedish bank in 1973; what shocked the public, though, was that several of the hostages bonded with the very thieves that had threatened to take their lives. Shortly after the release of the hostages, a few of them paid for the thieves' legal defense—and one even had a romantic relationship with one of the culprits. This syndrome has been psychologically applied to survivors of domestic abuse, war, and incest; but, the idea always seems foreign to many students. Bonding with a captor is a survival mechanism; and, perhaps the most notable case of the 20th Century in American culture concerns Patty Hearst.[8]

Christopher Castiglia's *Bound and Determined* ingeniously opens up the genre of "captivity narratives" to include fiction as well as memoirs; for instance, he includes Catherine Sedgwick's 19th Century romance novel *Hope Leslie* and Patty Heart's 20th Century memoir *Her Own Story*. Castiglia argues that captivity narratives engaged early American women readers with a world outside domestic boundaries; and additionally queered race and gender:

> Above all, I want to suggest that the captivity narratives hold their greatest interest...because they refuse to be static texts endorsing essential, unchanging identities and hence fixed social hierarchies of race and gender. Rather, the captivity narratives persistently explore generic and cultural changes, divisions, and differences occasioned by the captives' cultural crossings. (4)

Castiglia does not overtly name captivity narratives 'queer'; however, essentially, he argues that they are critiquing (the process of) normalization, which is a queer enterprise. In an attempt to vanquish the 'victim' status of the writers, Castiglia argues that the women captives are indeed feminist rebels and writing "in opposition to all men" (8). Castiglia argues that these texts' goals are to validate female agency and collectivity; however, I will argue that the purpose of the captivity narratives that I discuss is to articulate trauma as a confession in such a way that promotes witnessing—from readers of all sexes.

There are distinct reasons why the captivity narrative is evoked to describe trauma. One of those reasons is that the form lends itself to a critique of any attempt to distract readers from the confessional voice. Captivity narratives, like Rowlandson's, were literally enclosed with the words of respected men of the colony. For instance, Increase Mather is commonly thought to be the one who wrote the introduction to Rowlandson's narrative; and in that preface, he lauded the text as devotional and chastised anyone who could not find spiritual edification therein. And, Rowlandson's husband, a respected reverend, includes his sermons at the conclusion of the text itself. This strategy is comparable to the tactics used to validate both the moral uprightness and literary value of Anne Bradstreet when she published her collection of poetry; the testimonials, written by men, were almost as long as the poem compilation itself. These inclusions by male spectators have often been viewed as an indication of the lack of value that England Puritans assigned to women, their mental and creative abilities, and their other contributions to society. While colonial women were indeed thought to be inferior to men, these well respected testimonials of men may be operating within the text in ways that the authors did not anticipate. These inclusions also allowed an unpredicted and unprecedented space to emerge for American women: having received validation and written protection from the most prominent men in their society, they were rhetorically at liberty to discuss anything—including unspeakable traumas, their internal struggles, and even taboo subjects or behaviors.

A Queer Endeavor

From the very initial work on this project, I have thought that this project—like the texts that it analyzes—is quintessentially queer. I will not try to clearly define 'queer' because to attempt to do so would negate the innate objective of 'queering'. 'Queer' troubles both definition and conceptualization of normative concepts; and my project does not attempt to make 'queer' more normative and less 'queer', as it would be. In *Tendencies*, Eve Kosofsky Sedgwick discusses the significance of keeping 'queer' troubling, undefined, resistant—and, well, 'queer':

> Queer is a continuing moment, movement, motive—recurrent, eddying, *troublant*. The word 'queer' itself means *across*—it comes from the Indo-European root *twerkw*, which also yields the German *quer* (transverse), Latin *torquere* (to twist), English *athwart...queer...*is...multiply transitive. The immemorial current that queer represents is anitseparatist as it is antiassimilationist. Keenly, it is relational, and strange. (xii)

And, indeed, American women's confessional writing intentionally traverses across boundaries and queers them; examples of some of these boundaries are public/private, confession/silence, and even genres. While I will be arguing that some of the protagonists display queer desires, 'queer' encompasses more than sexuality—it provides a lens with which to engage the world. In *Fear of a Queer Planet*, Michael Warner writes:

> Every person who comes to a queer self-understanding knows in one way or another that her stigmatization is connected with gender, the family, notions of individual freedom, the state, public speech, consumption and desire, nature and culture, maturation, truth and trust, censorship, intimate life and social display, terror and violence, health care, and deep cultural norms about the bearing of the body. Being queer means fighting about these issues all the time, locally and piecemeal but always with consequences. (xiii)

I will be arguing that the authors of the memoirs, and the protagonists in the novels, embrace queer identities as a means to validate their agency—and to combat the potential for trauma to erase or replace it.

Like Showalter, I am not arguing that the tradition of American women's literature that I trace is held firmly together by the authors' "sexual difference" (xv). I struggled with the adjectives "feminist", "woman-centric", and "womanist"[9] and never could completely resolve myself to any of them. I believe that this project hearkens to feminism's emphasis on social change while evoking the spirit of personal woman-love inherent in Walker's womanism; but, this project also queers the binaries of gender and sex. And, the counter-publics do not restrict membership to only those who identify as 'woman'. In other words, all are welcome to witness—as long as they abide by the requirements of witnessing, validating and supporting. While this sounds like a space where all participants would softly hum 'kumbaya', that is not always the case. As many of the discussions within this project will reveal, this healing space is also a place to have impassioned exchanges.[10] Witnessing does not attempt to contain or appropriate emotions or reactions, which is why a counter-public must be conscientiously striving toward validation and support. Ann Cvetkovich posits, "Witnessing is fraught with ambivalence rather than fulfilling the melodramatic fantasy that the trauma survivor will finally tell all and receive the solace of being heard by a willing and supportive listener" (22). Cvetkovich argues that one must acknowledge "the burdens, the everydayness, and also the humor of witnessing" (22); and, in doing so, we claim the experiences of trauma as well as difficulties in articulating trauma as queer spaces.

Chapter 1 will explore the origin of this tradition, specifically within the early American texts Mary Rowlandson's 17th-Century *The Captivity and Restoration* of *Mrs. Mary Rowlandson* and Hannah Foster's 18th-Century seduction novel *The Coquette.* I believe that Rowlandson's captivity narrative is evoked within Foster's later novel, though with subtle differences; and, placing the two texts side-by-side reveals the subversive power of both texts that is generally not associated with early American texts or women. The cultural popularity of these texts, I believe, aided in their ability to provide an origin point for a tradition that continues today. Both texts, contrary to the mythology surrounding them, do not echo the severe religious dogma of the 17th and 18th centuries; in fact, both texts help re-imagine domestic spaces as wild, dangerous, and public. And, the texts inaugurate methods of queering boundaries—both cultural and linguistic—in order to confess trauma.

Chapter 2 focuses on Christine Jorgensen's *Autobiography* and Susanna Kaysen's *Girl, Interrupted,* which on the surface share a closer affiliation with Rowlandson's captivity narrative than Foster's novel. Both Jorgensen and Kaysen are held physically captive: Jorgensen, by her body, and Kaysen, by a mental institution. But these physical captivities are reinforced—if not created— by rhetorical captivities. Both memoirs explore the effects of normalizations of gender—as sources of trauma—on the corporeal body. Analyzing these two memoirs together help reveal the potential for re-inventing the case study as a subjective, but valid, space to articulate trauma; the two texts also highlight the possibility of archiving trauma by re-imagining the purpose of confession as witnessing the validation of agency.

Chapter 3 is a further exploration of how women's confessional literature traverses genres by placing Alice Walker's canonical text *The Color Purple* and Laurie Halse Anderson's *Speak* in dialogue with each other. Though both texts are fictional, the latter is a young adult novel; but both texts are highly disputed for their content—especially for young adult readers. The novels, both including the experience of living with the affects of rape, mirror *The Coquette* in diverse ways—including domesticity's potential to be a violent space. And, the texts also emphasizes the fact that traumatic experiences cannot be encapsulated by one event or experience; the continuation of traumatic experiences, via secondary wounding, highlights the imperativeness of a type of witnessing that validates and supports.

The afterward will suggest methods for enhancing our witnessing skills and creating a witnessing classroom. The road toward recovering and valuing American women's writing has been a difficult one—and it is still ongoing. And, I hope that this project will contribute to that journey, as well as to queer and trauma studies; and, as a teacher, I also hope that my project may alter the ways in which canonical texts, and less popular ones, by women writers are taught.

Notes

[1] F.O. Matthissen's *American Renaissance* was published in 1941 and is still hailed among literary critics. In approximately 700 pages, he addresses "the enduring requirements for great art" (xi) and applies them to notables (*all* white, Caucasian males), such as Emerson and Whitman. This literary history was, and continues to be, pivotal in the construction of the American literary canon.

[2] Several critics, notably Cathy Davidson, have been active in rediscovering early American women's texts (like Hannah Webster Foster's *The Coquette*) that were critical during the time in which they were published but have since then fallen into remote obscurity.

[3] For more information concerning these studies that discuss the PTSD symptoms found in rape survivors, see Dana Becker's *Through the Looking Glass*, especially pages 73-8, and Herman 28-32.

[4] I prefer the term "experiences" over "events" because, as I argue, I concentrate on the affective nature (versus bodily harm) of trauma. "Events" hint at a chronology of trauma, which I do not think can exist affectively.

[5] Since 1994, the American Psychiatric Association's DSM-IV has referred to Multiple Personality Disorder as Dissociative Identity Disorder.

[6] For a detailed and brilliant discussion on the United States' political goals and ability to maintain Guantanamo Bay, see Anne McClintock's "Paranoid Empire: Specters from Guantanamo and Abu Ghraib."

[7] Interestingly, as discussed in Chapter 3, the protagonist in *Speak* refers to her rapist only as "The Beast" and "It" through the first half of the novel.

[8] Patty Hearst, an American newspaper heiress, was abducted by The Symbionese Liberation Army in 1974 when she was 19 years old; she joined her captors in their movement and was captured by authorities after she helped them rob a bank in 1976. Even though her attorney argued that she had been brainwashed, physically assaulted, and sexually violated, she was sentenced to 35 years in prison. In 1982, she published her autobiography *Every Secret Thing*, which inspired fictional portrayal (and other subsequent documentaries). Her celebrity status brought her to the attention of President Jimmy Carter, who commuted her sentence after two years in prison, and President William Clinton—who pardoned her.

[9] For Alice Walker's definition of "womanism", see *In Search of Our Mother's Gardens,* xii. This topic will also be discussed further in Chapter 3 of this project.

[10] This is particularly important theme in Alice Walker's *The Color Purple*, discussed in Chapter 3.

Chapter 2: Reimagining Women's Literary History: Confessing Trauma in Mary Rowlandson's Captivity Narrative and Hannah Webster Foster's *The Coquette*

Rowlandson's *The Captivity and Restoration of Mrs. Mary Rowlandson* is the second known publication in the Americas by a woman[1]; published in 1682, her narrative sold widely in the Americas and England. The text chronicles Rowlandson's experience as a captive, in "removes," for the approximately three months she lived with Native American groups—particularly the Nipmucs, Narragansetts, and Wampanoags. During what is named Metacom's War (or King Philip's War), Indians[2] raided Rowlandson's village and captured she and her three children along with other villagers. Returned to her colony for a fee, Rowlandson waited over a decade to publish her account; but the public enthusiastically embraced her narrative. Hannah Webster Foster's *The Coquette* is an epistolary novel that was anonymously published in 1797, three years after another famous seduction novel, Susanna Rowson's *Charlotte Temple*.[3] *The Coquette*'s main protagonist is Eliza Wharton; after tending to her sickly father and fiancé, Eliza is free to seemingly enjoy her life. However, removed from the favor of her "friends" and labeled a reputable flirt, Eliza is forced into the company of a rake—who then rapes and impregnates her. And, typical of the traditional plot of the 'seduction novel', Eliza is forsaken by everyone and dies during childbirth with her shame.

Mary Rowlandson and Hannah Webster Foster wrote approximately a century apart, and they are virtually never discussed together because of the time gap and the assumption that their works belong to two distinct literary genres. Indeed, Mary Rowlandson's *The Captivity and Restoration of Mrs. Mary Rowlandson* and Hannah Webster Foster's *The Coquette* have been compartmentalized within literary history as historical and popular texts, and captivity narratives and seduction novels, respectively. Yet, these texts create origin points for American women's confessional writing. Trauma is expressed as confessions; these confessions include a tension between descriptions of suffering and silences; and an embrasure of queer identities, during and after captivity. This particular tradition of American women's confessional writing seeks to foster a counter-public that validates women's agency and traumas; and this tradition emerges, not so ironically, when women were thought to be spiritually and mentally inferior, and before trauma was a recognized discourse—much less recognized as being applicable to women's experiences.[4] Trauma, historically associated with survivors of war, was claimed as an experience by women who retain their agency as well as queer normalized constructions of gender, race, class, and desire. Because this tradition is so subversive, the majority of these texts have been regulated to particular genres that are assumed to have minimal literary and political merit. Both captivity narratives, originating in the 17th century, and seduction novels of the 18th century were (and are) thought to achieve similar purposes: to edify the spiritually righteous and to serve as a warning to those who defied cultural norms (and God along with them). But neither of these texts is simply devotional or morally pedagogical; rather, these texts operate in such a way that actively validates the significance of popular texts and subverts normalizations of gender and experiences of trauma.

Anthologies and some literary historians would have us believe that all captivity narratives, as well as seduction novels, are the same. Indeed, the plots from one captivity narrative or seduction novel to another appear to be comparable; however, not-so-subtle differences can be found between the texts. These differences include the agency that the survivors assume, the depictions of violence in relation to domesticity, the ways in which they confess, and even the ways they construct and create silences. For instance, a world of difference exists between Hannah Dunstan's and Rowlandson's captivity narrative; to begin, Dunstan's story is largely oral—originating and told as part of Cotton Mather's sermon—and was later dramatized in print with Mather's words, not Dunstan's. In Cotton Mather's account, Dunstan looses almost all of her humanity in becoming a super-hero, who almost single-handedly slaughters and scalps ten Indians while still in the process of recovering from childbirth.[5] Moreover, Rowlandson's narrative differs from many captivity narratives because it is composed in her own words, queers the domestic space, explicitly discusses the ambivalent feelings that she has toward her captors, and addresses life *after* she returns to her Puritan community. Likewise, *The Coquette* is assumed to be an example of a genre and not its own entity; contemporary critic Leonard Tennenhouse claims, "One cannot overstate the redundancy of these [seduction] novels" (1). There are, indeed, vast differences between Foster's *The Coquette* and other seduction novels—including William Brown's *The Power of Sympathy*, arguably the first seduction novel published in Colonial America. Foster's protagonist has agency, displays desire, and makes choices; however, the other female protagonists in seduction novels are a flat, immobile, and dispassionate portrait of a woman.[6] Furthermore, what remains different about *The Coquette* from other seduction novels is that: Foster actively seeks the companionship of her women friends—and prefers it to those of male attention; the protagonist's friends' dismissal of her (for more matronly tasks) that creates the situation for her "seduction"; and, an over-bearing moralistic narrator, typical of most novels of this time, is completely absent from the novel. Printed until the end of the 19th century, *The Coquette* and *Charlotte Temple* instigated cult followings among readers, who created and visited physical gravesites of the fictional protagonists; yet, these novels' popular appeal met with strict disapproval from ministers, literary reviewers, and even inventory librarians. This mass cultural acclaim, supplemented by censorship is a tradition that seems to follow most American women's confessional writings.

Problematizing Separate Sphere Ideology

While modern discourses of trauma and gender did not yet exist in the 17th and 18th centuries, literature and history emphasized the dire consequences of deviating from the "cult of domesticity." Reductively speaking, the cult of domesticity helped cement cultural expectations for women and contrasted the public space, which was gendered masculine. Domesticity continues to be associated with the familial home, a space inhabited by women that is stationary and tranquil. And, this rhetoric has been adopted by contemporary critics—most recognizable in "separate sphere ideology." Separate sphere ideology has been both helpful in recognizing the contributions of female writers but has also, simultaneously, solidified normalizations of gender and literary merit. Separate sphere ideology has been used by feminists, such as Ann

Douglas and Jane Tompkins, who seek to rediscover unacknowledged texts by women writers. In *The Feminization of American Culture* (first published in 1977), Ann Douglas argues that the end of the 18th century inaugurated a more feminine, less aesthetic, more passive philosophical type of literature: sentimental literature, which was for, by, and about women.[7] Jane Tompkins' *Sensational Designs* responds to Douglas' argument by showing how sentimental fiction and domesticity can, in fact, be political; so, while Tompkins solidifies separate sphere ideology even as she revises it.[8] Cathy Davidson and Jessamyn Hatcher argue that separate sphere ideology helps fuel feminist recovery projects that seek to include women in the literary canon[9]; but, Davidson and Hatcher also note that this ideology also solidifies binary notions of gender and the delusion that particular experiences can be "solely ascribed to the condition of being a 'woman'" (12). In *A Jury of Her Peers*, Elaine Showalter boldly presents the first literary history of American women's writing, which she argues emerges "from women's relation to the literary marketplace" (xv); implicit in Showalter's argument is that women's writing originated in reaction to a masculine tradition. In this project, though, I will argue that a distinct tradition of American women's writing emerges in order to articulate physical traumas as well as the traumas originating from normalizations of gender; and, this type of writing, I posit, is neither masculine or feminine— but queer. I do not wish to revise separate sphere ideology or the literary canon; rather, I intend to continue the process of queering the binary between private and public, which is also one of the aims of this rich tradition of American women's confessional writing. In both form and content, Rowlandson's and Foster's texts challenge separate sphere ideology, along with queering the domestic space and normalizations of gender.

The 17th and 18th centuries seemed to be a contradictory and treacherous time period for women navigating public recognition in America: on one hand, women were offered the potential for public success; and, on the other, crossing an invisible line of too much notoriety ended with fates that were often deadly. Early American women generally encountered ambivalence and suspicion toward their public speech and writing; for instance, Governor John Winthrop postulates that the masculine occupation of writing and reading could result in a woman's insanity:

> [a Mrs. Hopkins] was fallen into sad infirmity, the loss of her understanding and reason, which had been growing upon her diverse years, by occasion of her giving herself wholly to reading and writing ... If she had attended to her household affairs, and such things as belong to women, and not gone out of her way and calling to meddle such things as are proper for men, whose minds are stronger... she had kept her wits. (qtd. in Elderidge 372).

Another notable woman who chose "to meddle [with] such things as are proper for men" is Anne Hutchinson, who was excommunicated because she visibly engaged in the public sphere by leading her own discussion groups.[10] The first known publication was Anne Bradstreet's collection of poetry, only a few years earlier before Rowlandson's narrative. Bradstreet's literary success is exceptional because she was able to maintain her moral integrity as a governor's wife, a mother of eight children, and respectable Puritan. However, there are differences between the form of Bradstreet's and Rowlandson's narratives: Bradstreet's collection of poetry is prefaced with no fewer than twelve pages by notable men who profess her moral character and how her writing did not negatively affect her motherly or wifely duties; Rowlandson's text is introduced by a notable clergyman, generally assumed to be Increase Mather, and concludes with a sermon by her husband (another clergyman). Mather's introduction, though, is a visible example of how the text "anticipates the potential for hostility toward the woman writer" (Logan 262). In his preface, Mather defends the authenticity of Rowlandson's text by arguing that she is an respectable woman who is allowing him to thrust her writing into public view—and only for the edification of others: "Though this Gentlewoman's modesty would not thrust it [the narrative] into the Press, [...] Some Friends having obtained sight of it, could not be so much affected [...] as to judge it worthy of publick view [...] that God might have his due glory, and others benefit by it as well as herself" (qtd. in Rowlandson 29). While Rowlandson's text does include two separate pieces from clergymen, these additions contrast the inundation of masculine voices in Bradstreet's book that comprise nearly half the book. Thus, Rowlandson's own words easily comprised the bulk of the text; and, the in doing so, her work becomes a critical point in women's literary history. Although Foster's novel was published almost a century from Rowlandson's narrative, similar ideas about public space and women writers existed. Foster reacted to this position by publishing the novel anonymously. Foster's novel, also entitled "The History of Eliza Wharton", had the genuine appearance of a memoir instead of a piece of fiction; and without an omnipresent, like most novels of the time, Foster's text explicitly challenges the differences between 'fiction' and 'the real.'

Even though they suffered ridicule as "scribbling women" and public censure, women continued to write—and successfully publish—many types of literature, including: poems, letters, poetry, journals, diaries, household manuals, travelogues, captivity and slave narratives, and novels. The increasing visibility of women writers created a crisis for men of letters, who responded by creating a distinction between the import of literary and political texts by male authors and sensational texts, which were largely written by women; and, this distinction between literary or historical (belonging to the public sphere) and popular (belonging to the private sphere) continues with modern criticism. Feminist critics such as Jane Tompkins have attempted "opening up the canon" by recognizing the importance of women's texts previously unacknowledged as politically and culturally significant. Politicizing texts ignored in F.O. Matthissen's celebrated literary history *American Renaissance*, Tompkins recognizes the contradiction between democracy and the exclusion of those previously acknowledged texts that seek to "redefine the social order" (xi) by reaching and influencing the masses. Cathy Davidson explains the importance of the novel following the Revolution and notes that the novel "creates its own truth by involving the reader in the process of that creation" (*Revolution* 52). Mikhail M. Bakhtin writes that the novel's ability to privilege the reader in the art of creation allows the novel and reader to avoid categorization: "The novel, after all, has no canon of its own. It is, by its nature, not canonic. It is plasticity itself. It is a genre that is ever questing, ever examining itself and subjecting its established forms to review" (qtd. in Davidson *Revolution* 44). What is peculiar of the novel, as Davidson views it, is its politicized marginalization within American discourse as trivial and even morally corrupt—and yet, the novel sold and affected masses no less than pamphlets from the Federalists.

Rowlandson's text is generally afforded historical merit and heavily anthologized, but it is certainly not considered literary or canonical in the way that Nathaniel Hawthorne's *The Scarlett Letter* is. Foster's novel, however is (and was) considered unequivocally "popular" and virtually without any merit—literary or otherwise. Rowlandson's text is one such example of literature written by a woman that was embraced by the masses upon publication; yet, Foster's novel, only a couple of years later earned simultaneous cultural acclaim and censorship—and has faded almost into oblivion these days, except for its shadow. One might postulate that the varying responses to these texts reflected ideas about novels—or fiction— that surfaced in the 18th Century. In the 18th century, sentimental fiction was the most widely read genre; while the burgeoning middle class— teachers, doctors, clerks, and the masses—composed the vast readership, it was still assumed to be popular and without literary merit.[11] Sentimentality and sensationalism are still viewed as low-brow entertainment and composed of a largely female audience. Indeed, readers who read Rowlandson's and (especially) Foster's text were more than likely to shed tears and have genuine affective responses to plots that may seem too dramatic by modern assessments; they viewed novels like *The Coquette* as not being situated within "the realm of fairy tale or escapist fantasy, but in the very bedrock of reality" (Tompkins 127).[12] That is: strictly speaking, sensationalism does not involve a sadomasochistic voyeur who revels in the unfortunate protagonists' predicaments. Rather, sentimental fiction provided an avenue for readers to commune over "real"

experiences that were difficult, if not impossible, to speak openly about—
and to have emotional responses that were considered both logical and
often patriotic. Literally read to rags, copies of *The Coquette* and similar
novels were thought to be potentially dangerous to a woman's fragile mind.
The Coquette responds to this crisis of the emerging readership of
women's sentimental fiction by explicitly arguing that women's confessional
writings may be sensational—but they are steeped in fact, neither in myth
nor female fantasy. *The Coquette* was based on a particular woman's
experience: Eliza Whitman, a poet, had an affair and eventually gave birth
to a stillborn baby while dying. News of Whitman spread through the
normal channels of oral and written communication; and, upon the
publication of *The Coquette*, readers noticed the parallels between
Whitman and the fictional Eliza, who shared the same monogram—"Eliza
Wharton." The 'realness' of experiences are at the heart of the popularity
of both Rowlandson's and Foster's texts—helping to create an intimate
bond between the narrative voices and the readers.

The Wild(er)ness of Domesticity

The popularity of Rowlandson's and Foster's texts helped transform the
literary landscape for women writers by virtue of how they deviated from
relying on male validation for authenticity. But, I do not believe that the
distinction of popular versus historical or literary texts originated solely in
reaction to the author's sex. Rather, I believe that the subversive content
of Rowlandson's and Foster's novels is the major reason that these texts
were considered a political threat and, thus, de-politicized from the
beginning as "popular" entertainment. Rowlandson's and Foster's texts are

overtly political in content, which may even be one of the reasons that the middle-class (who would benefit from a revisions to aristocratic hegemony) eagerly read them. These texts engage in discussions that were both political and everyday experiences; the experiences of Rowlandson and Eliza were both easy for readers to envision because they were familiar points of mass discussion—but also because they included personal struggles with popular ideologies and normalizations.

Rowlandson's and Foster's texts do not shy away from "personal" experiences that were considered taboo—experiences such as traveling every day in proximity to political enemies and a lower-class girl enjoying the attention of high-class society for a short time. These inclusions of generally forbidden subjects are indeed considered as confessions by readers, just as they are today, because the narrator must confess to how she reacted to these illicit situations. For instance, Rowlandson and Eliza are surprised by their own reactions at scenes of danger. Both narratives begin with the heroines being surrounded by the devastating effects of death; the difference is that Rowlandson recognizes that she is brought into captivity whereas Eliza is disillusioned into thinking that she has just been released from domestic captivity. Rowlandson begins her narrative with images of blood and gore, bodies ghastly mutilated and property destroyed by both Indians and colonists. Repeated she watched bodies being mutilated; in one instance she remarks, they [Indians] "knock'd him on the head, stripped him naked, and split open his bowels" (Rowlandson 31). The events that Rowlandson accounts are by no means romanticized. Rowlandson encounters her own fears of death; she confesses: "I had often before this said, that if the Indians should come, I should chuse rather to be killed by them than taken alive; but when it came to the trial my mind changed; their glittering Weapons so daunted my spirit" (33). This admittance of fear attests to gravity of the situation and the narrative voice's memory of a past self and the power of trauma to alter convictions. When *The Coquette* begins, Eliza has spent a large portion of her youth attending to both her ill father and the fiancé, who was chosen by her father and strikingly resembles him. Eliza nurses them until they are both no longer living—at which she exclaims, "An unusual sensation possesses my breast; a sensation which I thought could never pervaded it on any occasion what ever. It is pleasure" (Foster 5). She is seemingly reacquainted with joy by being liberated from years spent in a house filled with somberness and death. Quite simply, she thinks she now has the opportunity to *live* and be the mistress of her own fate. Eliza's reaction seems cold and callous; but, unbeknownst to her, she is in just as much danger as Rowlandson. Without a father and a husband, this clergyman's daughter does not have the financial means to survive alone—at least in the comfortable manner to which she is accustomed—in 18th century America.

Domesticity, itself, is presented vastly different in Rowlandson's and Foster's texts than in the cult of domesticity—or even modern discussions. Rowlandson and Foster present domesticity as a public and potentially violent space, which is neither feminine nor masculine. In fact, the line between domesticity and wilderness is imprecise from the beginning of Rowlandson's narrative: while we may think of the Indian raid as a clearly defined invasion into the American and domestic sphere, Rowlandson's "home" was actually *in* "the wilderness"—both literally and figuratively.

Rowlandson's, more than likely, saw the physical formation of her house amidst the strange and foreign land. But that construction did not keep the "wilderness" at bay; the wilderness visibly existed no further than behind the newly erected buildings and threatened to invade them. And, the stableness of towns, which contrasted the natives' nomadic traditions, made the colonists an easy target for invasions and destructions of those symbols of British superiority. Thus, the colonists most likely envisioned their homes—this domestic space—as potentially dangerous areas and subject to unpredictable violence. In "Manifest Domesticity," Amy Kaplan explores the interconnectedness of the rhetoric of domesticity and colonial expansion. Domesticity, Kaplan argues, is always "in intimate opposition to the foreign" (183) and is imagined as both the familial household and the nation as a home. Thus, Kaplan argues that "we should think of domesticity not as a static condition but as the process of domestication, which entails conquering and taming the wild, the natural, and the alien" (184).

The process of domestication and the space of domesticity, then, is not "natural"—but constructed. Thus, colonization can, and does, occur from within. For those, then, who are forced to adhere to normalizations, this "familiar" domestic space can be defined as a captive space—one that contains and appropriates differences—even for supposed "natives." Captivity provides us with a discourse to discuss normalizations, which can be traumatic and rationalize physical violence. Normalizations of gender, for instance, are just one of the many ways in which violence against women and children are perpetuated; gendered feminine and weak, women and children are continually culturally and economically reminded of their inferiority. These accepted normalizations set-up, if not promote, domestic violence against women and children. Indeed, Herman's *Trauma and Recovery*[13] is an important project because it creates awareness to the experiences of the "domestic captivity of women and children [which] is often unseen" (74). Herman makes a distinction between one experience of trauma and a succession of experiences: "A single traumatic event can occur almost anywhere. Prolonged, repeated trauma, by contrast occurs only in circumstances of captivity" (74).[14] Because Rowlandson was a prisoner of war, it seems understandable that she suffers trauma by virtue of her physical captivity; however, the very genre "seduction novels" does little to indicate the violence that lies therein. 'Seduction' is a word that is both pleasing to the ear and romantic in intonations; however, within these 'seduction novels', young women were kidnapped, raped, made to suffer alone and in poverty, and finally forced to die in childbirth with (and, arguably, because of) dishonor. The main protagonist in *The Coquette*, Eliza Wharton, is rejected by high society because of her lowly class, refusal to marry within her class, and homosocial desires; finally imprisoned in her mother's domestic space, she becomes prey to a rapist, who forsakes her while she suffers her (and her child's) fatal end. In this way, we can see that Rowlandson is a captive of Puritanical dogma and normalizations of gender; and, Eliza is held captive by normalizations of gender, class, and heterosexual desire.

In fact the very notion of "seduction novels" as a genre intimates that the protagonist's passivity and inability to discern a foe results in her tragic demise. If the women in 'seduction novels' are indeed *seduced*, it is by the false sense of protection from other women in the novel. While her

43

"friends" did not create those normalizations, they have adequate reason to reinforce them; so, while they may not be considered Eliza's captors, they are certainly (at least) her guards. Viewing Eliza's female friends as her captors—or at least guards—elucidates the inequality between Eliza and her 'friends.' Eliza is surrounded by women who are either married or on the verge of marriage and who want to "repose in safety" (Foster 24); and Eliza's eagerness to participate in society is perceived as a burden. Eliza is a burden to her friends primarily because of her class status, which requires her friends to be proactive in Eliza's life. For instance, Eliza relies on them for invitations to social gatherings, recreational outings, and such. She is a "pensioner of friendship" (Foster 36), required to rely on others for amusements and female companionship because she does not have the financial means to reciprocate their social invitations. Eliza pens the vast majority of letters between female characters because writing letters is a diversion that is financially available to her. Eliza writes eight letters before receiving a response from her closest friend Lucy; in that eighth letter, Eliza acknowledges her fear that her friends are "so weary of my company, as to wish to dispose of me" (Foster 24) via marriage; she bemoans that "Marriage is the tomb of friendship. It appears to me a very selfish state" (Foster 24). Indeed, Eliza's rebuke—instead of genuine care for her friend—could be interpreted as the sole motivation for her 'friend's' eventual reply. After her death, her female friends proclaim their dead friend as "happy" (Foster 169). In *An Archive of Feelings*, Ann Cvetkovich argues that trauma can be exploited as "wound" to heal in the name of unity[15]; while Cvetkovich discusses this unity in terms of patriotism, I think her theory is apt here—in relation to the normalization of gender, desire, and class. At the end of the novel, as all of Eliza's "friends" surround her tomb, I have the eerie feeling that they all played their parts in putting there. Like a blemish, Eliza had not married and continued with her flirty ways toward men—but all the while only wanting the company of her economically secure female friends. She needed to be erased—for a seamless appearance of unity.

Captivity: A Discourse of Trauma

The discourse of captivity is an especially effective avenue to articulate trauma for several reasons. For instance, a captive is kidnapped and held hostage by visible and physical barriers (such as wired fences); but, captivity is mostly preserved by a myriad of emotional and psychological threats, fears, and alliances. Captors' reliance on invisible mechanisms helps them to maintain control over the subject for elongated amounts of time and across territorial boundaries; for this reason, captivity is both a physical state of being as well as a state of consciousness that can continue well after one is separated from one's captor. The intimate relationship that develops between the captive and captor is one of ambivalence; for this reason, the captive feels both loyal and fearful of the very persons (and even ideologies) that restrain and violate her. Instead of hiding the intricate and contradictory ways that captivity and trauma affects one's feelings towards others and one's self, both Rowlandson and Foster explore queer positionality as a way to acknowledge the internal conflicts and guilt that trauma survivors feel. Acknowledging these invisible methods of control and captivity is an important step in transforming the way we envision trauma. Trauma, like captivity, is often invisible to the naked eye—making it more dangerous because "it often leaves no sign of a problem" (Cvetkovich 46). Trauma, composed of both physical and psychological pain, "does not simply resist language but actively destroys it" (Scarry 4). So, Rowlandson and Foster were forced to find inventive ways for making trauma obvious to their readers. While Rowlandson inserts biblical quotations to fill gaps of trauma, Foster incorporates variations of silences.

The biblical quotations used throughout Rowlandson's narrative are generally interpreted as being further support that her narrative voice is subjugated by dogma and the masculine voice of Mather. Furthermore, the quotations are often seen as Rowlandson's attempt to integrate herself back into her community—to regain the status she had before being held captive. Kathryn Zabelle Derounian argues:

> Immediately after her captivity, Rowlandson suffered from psychological trauma similar to what we now term the "survivor syndrome," but that she tried to minimize the symptoms to conform to the Puritan doctrine of providential affliction. In writing her captivity account, Rowlandson therefore performed a personal and public service. Articulating her experiences was therapeutic (personal) because she confronted her past journey outside conventional society, yet it was also devotional (public) because she documented her present reentry in it. ("Publication, Promotion," 240)

I believe that the biblical excerpts do not control the narrative as much as they augment the narrator's sentiments; when devoid of any way to articulate what she is seeing and feeling, Rowlandson uses the power of affect associated with the biblical references as a communicative tool. She is not allowing the scriptures to replace her voice; rather, she is inserting

46

her ineffable religious convictions and experiences where utterances of an indefinable experience of captivity would otherwise be. Reading biblical scriptures within her narrative as visible marks of trauma is quite different than interpreting them as policing her experiences. For instance, on "The Fourth Remove", Rowlandson writes: "I cannot express to main the affliction that lay upon my spirit; but the Lord helped me at that time to express it to himself. I opened my Bible to read, and the lord brought that precious Scripture to me" (39). Looking for an understandable translation of her feelings, she resorts to a commonality between herself and her readers: the bible. Rowlandson's affinity for the scripture is not merely of 'fact,' either; rather, she relates to the words as more than words: "Many and many a time have I sate down and wept sweetly over this Scripture" (39). Unable to express all of her experiences and emotions, she does not allow herself to be rendered silent; rather, she inserts biblical in order to render trauma visible to her audience.

While Rowlandson engages and resists Puritan doctrine, Foster's text must struggle with the discourse of sympathy. During the early American republic, sympathy was lauded as the ultimate expression of humanity. To be capable of feeling for another's plight was considered tantamount to physical exertions that would alleviate the person's sufferings. The power of sympathy was thought to create unambiguous unity, an ideal social fabric and civil society. Yet, to create this idealized collectivity, the brutal forces of coercion and erasure were embraced in order to substantiate an impression of unity. This sort of affective power could mend the gaps of a new republic riddled with differences of race and class; and conveniently, this logic precludes the necessity of challenging the constructions of race,

47

class, and even gender to alter the material circumstances that specific individuals struggle with. Particularly, female sympathy has been esteemed by literary and social critics as visible evidence of a powerful, and oftentimes subversive, community of women in the early republic. Eliza's voice, one of obligation "both [by] nature and education" (Foster 5) to her parents, reveals Eliza as a dutiful daughter and member of her community; the traumas of, and her willingness to tend to her ill fiancé, and the death of her father—all of these situations create sympathy for the heroine whose fate the reader expects to be disastrous. In *The Politics of Sympathy*, Elizabeth Barnes writes, "sympathy is made safe, and readers are encouraged to imagine a harmonious rather than a disjunctive relationship between their own desires and that which is desired for them by a protective parent" (18). Thus Barnes is attentive to the notion that the language of sympathy allows the readers to morally judge the deceased heroine without consequence. In *Critical Fictions: Sentiment and the American Market, 1780-1870,* Joseph Fitchenberg argues that the language of sympathy emerges in order to counter the language of "humanity", which "is the virtue of a woman" (John Smith, qtd. in Fitchenberg 74). According to Fitchenberg, "Sympathy was the ability to moderate feeling, to control one's responses as to achieve the precise balance, the perfect pitch, that would secure social concord" (74). This "social concord", of course, particularly involved economics and the exchange of commodities; Fitchenberg observes that the language of commercialism found itself in the very discourse of sympathy: "exchanging feeling is itself a market mechanism" (78).

Foster uses silences in two ways, which becomes more pronounced with comparing her novel with previous seduction novels. Firstly, Foster does not include a narrator who inscribes meaning on the text; and, after her rape, she also allows Eliza to remain quiet instead of perpetually begging for forgiveness. The absence of militant masculine voices—like Mather in Rowlandson's narrative or the narrator in *Charlotte Temple*—creates an intimate relationship with the reader. A preface by a male figure, defending the authenticity of the work or the author, was normally not included in sensational novels—and is thusly missing from *The Coquette*. The text also lacks other attributes that are customary for the genre of seduction novels: a preface from the author and an omniscient narrator. For instance, the function of the authorial preface in Susanna Rowson's *Charlotte Temple* (which was published only a few years before Foster's novel) operates much like Mather's preface in Rowlandson's text; the difference is, of course, that the preface is written by a female author. Regardless, the purpose of the text is not literary but moral pedagogy "for the perusal of the young and thoughtless of the fair sex" (Rowson xlix). This obvious instruction continues within the text's omniscient narrator who instructs readers how to remain a dutiful and virtuous daughter by obeying her parents. This omniscient narrator also serves another purpose: to speak for the heroine after she becomes invisible; Foster's text uniquely allows the heroine's voice to fall *explicitly* silent. The absence of those overbearing voices in Foster's novel does not instruct the reader what to think or feel; rather, it takes great risks in making Eliza's silences explicitly obvious. Tracing the origin of Eliza's silence, then, becomes the goal in order to locate the point where she becomes a witness to her own life— much like Rowlandson.

Arguably, her peers attempt to silence Eliza from the beginning by creating the context of her life; after having dutifully cared for her father and her fiancé as they fell ill, the young lady is then encouraged to marry and commit her life to another man—who is another clergyman named Mr. Boyer. Attempts to silence Eliza exist after her rape, to be sure; but, her "friends" attempt to silence her from the beginning. From the onset of the novel, Eliza "wish[es] for no other connection than that of friendship" (Foster 6). Letter after letter, she implores Lucy to "write soon, and often" (Foster 6), even proclaiming her eternal devotion: "whatever my fate may be, I shall always continue your Eliza Wharton" (Foster 9). Solitariness is not enough to induce Eliza to accept Boyer's marriage proposal until after her best friend Lucy is married. While others are enjoying the felicity of Lucy's marriage, Eliza explains her uncharacteristic silence and depressed spirits to Boyer: "She [Lucy] has conferred upon another that affection which I wished to engross. My love was too fervent to admit a rival" (Foster 70). Lucy's nuptials, then, shatter Eliza's last hopes for being forever united with her beloved friend; thereafter, she is traumatized by the devastation of her romantic sensibilities toward Lucy. After her friends are married, she returns to her mother's home—where she is "seduced." Indeed, the withdrawal of female companionship is what induces Eliza to "embraced [sic] with avidity the consoling power of friendship, ensnaringly offered by my [her] seducer [Sanford]" (Foster 143). Eliza's letters are sparser and grow more frantic until her final letter, which is imbued with clarity and resolve—and perhaps, relief. Davidson interprets Eliza's silence at the end of the novel to be emblematic of her victimization and lack of freedom—symptoms of having no agency; Davidson writes that Eliza cannot escape her fate, that she only exists: "Eliza [is] faced not with a freedom of choice but an absence of suitors […] Eliza naively sought to exercise her freedom only to learn that she had none" (146). Elizabeth Maddock Dillon adds to Davidson's framework that Eliza does not have choices—that she is tragically fated, reinforcing the lack of rights allotted to women; Dillon argues that Eliza "fatally misunderstands this social space as open rather than closed, as productive and creative rather than dedicated to procuring a temporal narrative (path) linking private to public and gendering her body through heterosexual marriage" (187). But, I wish to distinguish the silence as language's inability to articulate the depth of her sufferings and the author's lack of condemnation for Eliza. Like Rowlandson, Eliza is bound by the cultural expectations of gender and cult of domesticity; but, I believe that Eliza's ultimate demise is facilitated by her lower class and illusion that all women are unified.

Eliza's trauma is largely unrecognized in criticism because political and erotic alliances between women are often ignored and because of the desire to see all women—readers and protagonists—aligned with each other. Eliza is haunted by her visibly diminishing circle of friends after Boyer flees from her: "The agitating scenes, through which I have lately passed, have broken my spirits and rendered me unfit for society" (Foster 98). She no longer feels capable of transcending her anguish, evidence that she is experiencing the effects of trauma. If Eliza's characteristic silence is interpreted as the effects of trauma, her agency remains intact and the appropriation of her narrative becomes more visible. Instead of reforming her romantic relationship with Eliza, she objectifies and bullies Eliza. For instance, after Eliza's attempt to place her anguish into language, Lucy rejoinders: "Your truly romantic letter came safe to hand.

Indeed, my dear, it would make a very pretty figure in a novel. A bleeding heart, slighted love, and all the *et ceteras* of romance, inter into the composition!" (Foster 107). I have argued that the beginning of the novel shows Lucy's inscription of Eliza's fate; and this later example is further evidence that Lucy feels superior to Eliza—that she has the power to script Eliza's life.

Eliza insists that she wants to experience the same sympathy that she has bestows on others and be "benevolent to all around me, [and] I wish for no other connection than of friendship" (6). And, this is exactly what is denied. In "Sisterhood in a Separate Sphere," Claire C. Pettengill explores the didactic relationships in the female community, "the tightly knit circle of women which supports, encourages, protects and provides for Eliza, even as it scolds and criticizes her" (186). Pettengill writes about the bonds of friendship, which seem to be virtually unbroken during Eliza's demise:

> Ironically, Eliza's friends continue busily to communicate with one
> another for and about Eliza. When she stops writing, her
> conversations and actions are reported at second hand, passed
> around from friend to friend. They constantly urge Eliza to write—to
> rejoin the circle. After she "falls," they consider her redeemed,
> because of the penitence she reveals in her confessions…Most
> important, in the eyes of Julia, are the "scraps of writing" Eliza leaves
> behind at her death. (198)

However, Eliza is actively secluded by her friends—she is scripted, by her friends, as a coquette and fated before she acts, not out of choice, but the lack thereof. Along with ignoring women's involvement in the demise of their own sex, critics also erase the other female characters in entirety. For instance, Tennenhouse claims that American seduction tales are only pawns in a game of power among men: "Women in these American stories are the unvarnished medium for carrying on a relationship among men" (9). This theory falters especially in regard to *The Coquette* because Eliza's father dies in the beginning of the novel; thus, no conversation by patriarchs about Eliza appears. While someone may claim that Eliza's lack of a father is the reason why she does not survive, homosocial desire and socioeconomics seems like a more valid reason. Tennenhouse also notes, "Once his [Sanford's] economic needs have been met by a well-made marriage, Sanford is free to pursue his sexual desires elsewhere" (12). Because Sanford continues to appear to be wealthy (though he is secretly in debt), he is able to mercenarily marry a wealthy woman; but, Eliza neither has the means nor desires to deceive others concerning her finances in order to capture a "well-made marriage." While it is easy to bemoan Eliza's fate, I am always saddened that she never even realized that she had been born in captivity—and never escaped it.

While one might recommend that Eliza's homoerotic vision is her tragic flaw, such a claim would quickly return to a discussion of economics: if Eliza was allotted some fortune or a trade, she could have continued her social life and romantic friendships. In "A Mob of Lusty Villagers," Elizabeth Dill discusses the domestic space as an instigator of seduction, arguing that Eliza's social death precedes her physical death: "It is *after* Eliza's return home, however, that her seduction is completed, and it is as a scene for sexuality and ruin that the home *sustains* rather than subverts the seduction" (258). And, Eliza's socioeconomic situation is precisely what forces her to return to—and remain in—her mother's domestic sphere.

Eliza appears to seek refuge from the pretenses of society, but she finds her mother is unable to provide adequate sanctuary; had Eliza possessed an alternative abode, financial means to travel in other social circles and form new relationships, her fate may have been different. Likewise, if Eliza had been willing to fall in social status, she may have averted her fate. To keep from falling in the social ladder, Eliza does not search out a trade or skill by which she can support herself—nor does she seek out a community of women in working classes who are invested in romantic friendships. Falling in social status is not an option for Eliza because she refuses to engage in any activity that would create more barriers between herself and Lucy. Because she chooses to "closet" herself within the confines of her mothers' abode, she forsakes her utopian vision of collectivity between women. It is this "closeting" of desire and benevolence that the text does not validate; Eliza's hermit-like existence constitutes her demise more than any other choice. A spurned and traumatized lover, Eliza secludes herself like the other female characters only to find that she lacks the skills and fortune to acquire safety and happiness within the domestic realm.

Lucy's situation provides readers with an alternative to Eliza's situation: Lucy's wealth and marriage provides her with avenues to form new romantic attachments with other females, namely Julia Granby. After Boyer's final rejection, Eliza realizes that she must marry Sanford in order to be able to circulate in the same circles as Lucy; she writes to Lucy, "I stand in need of the consoling power of friendship" (Foster 100). Acknowledging that she cannot possess Lucy as she previously envisioned, Eliza requests a 'living miniature'—or version—of her in hopes that she may recover from her devastated hopes:

54

Oh that you were near me, as formally, to share and alleviate my
cares! ...Such a one, next to yourself, I think Julia Granby to be. With
your leave and consent I should esteem it a special favor if she would
come and spend a few months with me...If I have not forfeited your
friendship, my dear Mrs. Sumner, write to me, and pour its healing
balm in the wounded mind of your Eliza Wharton. (Foster 106)

Eliza must rely on Lucy, though, to procure this request. Lucy's social
status affords her the ability to form bonds with young ladies and direct
their futures. The ability to share an intimate bond with another woman,
then, appears to rely upon wealth—and perhaps the security of marriage.
Lucy does consent to parting with Julia and Eliza later refers to Julia as "My
Julia" (Foster 108), as if battling for the possession of Julia's affections.
Quite possibly, Eliza is trying to capture the adoration of Julia in order to
ease the pain left by Lucy's unreciprocated love, or Eliza is attempting to
spark jealousy within Lucy. Regardless, Eliza does not make her person or
feelings accessible to Julia until she is certain of her disastrous fate and
immanent need for friendship/sympathy.

Rowlandson's reactions toward her captors are more customarily
ambivalent than Eliza's; her feelings are a combination of fear, loyalty,
admiration, and hate. Rowlandson, unlike Eliza, does not initially describe
her captors as unequivocal "friends;" however, she does become
accustomed to her environment and even acknowledges some of her
captors as friends. Rowlandson's descriptions of Native Americans are
comparable to other white, middle-class colonists and appear throughout
her narrative: "those black creatures in the night" (33) and "ravenous
Bears" (33). These portrayals of natives make it easy to understand how

colonists justified both violence against and the desire to convert the native inhabitants—as well as 'domesticate' the land. However, in Rowlandson's narrative, she visibly struggles with depicting her captors as savages and humans—mirroring her own internal struggle to both identify with and in opposition of her captors. At one point she admits that her master is "the best friend that I had…in both cold and hunger" (46). Rowlandson speaks of acclimation to her captor's environment, not so ironically, by discussing 'taste':

> The first week of my being among them I hardly eat any thing; the second week I found my stomach grow very faint for want of something; and yet 'twas very hard to get down their filthy trash; but the third week (though I could think how formerly my stomach would turn against this or that, and I could starve and die before I could eat such things, yet) they were pleasant and savoury to my taste. (40)

Rowlandson's regard for her captor's food is emblematic of how she is forced to cultivate certain desires—for survival—that would have otherwise repulsed her. Rowlandson also notices the queerness in her own behavior regarding death: "I cannot take but notice how, at another time, I could not ber to be in the room where any dead person was; but now the case is changed; I must and could lye down by my dead Babe, side by side, all the night after" (36). These changes and acclimations may not be so surprising when we more closely analyze Rowlandson's positions within Puritan society and among the Indians.

In *Bound and Determined*, Christopher Castiglia writes that captivity narratives provide the opportunity for "white women… [to] demonstrate

skills and attitudes of which their home cultures thought them incapable"
(4). Elaine Showalter claims that captivity narratives "described women's
abilities to survive and endure through stoicism and resourcefulness;
experimented with personal confession" (14). Indeed, Rowlandson
survives harsh conditions and travels in ways that she is unaccustomed;
these experiences sharply contrast the expectations placed upon those of
her sex, gender, and class. For instance, Rowlandson candidly describes
the carnage that she witnesses when Indians raid her village, her wavering
committal to death in the face of captivity, the death of her child in her
arms, the lack of sexual imprudence toward her, and her assimilation into
her captor's culture before returning to her Puritan community. I theorize,
based on Rowlandson's acclimation to her captors' environment, that her
"resourcefulness" (Showalter 14) includes recognizing domestic space
within the confines of captivity and ultimately embracing a queer identity.
Her acclimation was so intense that she would often forget that she was in
captivity:

> Cannot but remember how many times sitting in their wigwams, and
> musing on things past, I should suddenly leap up and run out, as if I
> had been at home, forgetting where I was, and what my condition
> was; but when I was without, and saw nothing but wilderness, and
> woods, and a company of barbarous heathens, my mind quickly
> returned to me. (Rowlandson 47)

Rowlandson is provided with opportunities to runaway—several times
while moving between wigwams to visit her son and also when an Indian
couple offers to help her escape.[16] While some may argue that she does
not attempt to flee because of her "learned passivity" as a Puritan woman, I
think that the reason is that she sees her survival intimately connected with

her captors and thusly has built a pseudo-home—a familial relation—that contrasted "the wilderness" that she would be forced to encounter if she ventured away. I do not intend to devalue Rowlandson's positionality as someone who is held physically captive with threats of violence or imply that this "pseudo-home" was a happy one. My students often point out the fact that Rowlandson may have fared better—or, at least, she may have had more immediate liberties—with the Indians than within Puritan society. This is evident by the fact that Rowlandson even profits within her captor's society, using her sewing industry to accrue money and food as an independent woman.[17] But, even then, she feels compelled to share her earnings with the Indian who "has taken her into his household. For instance, Rowlandson employs her sewing industry and is rewarded with a knife, which she eagerly gives to her 'master' (the head of the wigwam where she lives); "I was not a little glad that I had any thing that they would accept of, and be pleased with" (44). And, indeed, the tension between Rowlandson and her captors does dissipate from time to time; she mentions that particular individuals are "very kind to me" (44) and she recognizes their humanity.

Some critics, like Jill Lepore, believe that Rowlandson believed in the healing power of written confession: "Mary Rowlandson wrote her way out of captivity and back into the Christian, English fold, freeing herself from memories of life among savages" (148). However, I agree with Bryce Traister, who positions Rowlandson's narrative as secular and confessional; like Traister, I have claimed that Rowlandson retains control over her text and depicts "personal suffering [that] stubbornly resists its translation into the Protestant allegory of divinely appointed affliction" (325).

As a wife of a well respected minister, and a later a widow, her chastity and allegiance to Puritan ideals are important to her status within her community. For instance she acknowledges the curiosity about her sexual behaviors while captive:

> I have been in the midst of those...that feared neither God, nor man, nor the devil...sleeping all sorts together, and not one of them ever offered me the least abuse of unchastity to me, in word or action. Though some are ready to say I speak it for my own credit; but I speak it in the presence of God, and to His Glory. (Rowlandson 61)

Rowlandson does not explain why she was left 'undefiled' by those she names barbaric and demonic; she does not claim that her own visible virtues deterred her captors from hurting her; rather, she attests that supernatural power protected her that defies her logic and comprehension. One motivation for this confession is, of course, so that she can more easily integrate herself back into the folds of her community. Two other possibilities are less readily acknowledged: her fear of secondary wounding and desire to protect her captors from malicious accusations.[18] Survivors of trauma can be traumatized (again) by others' negative responses to their narratives. Rowlandson anticipates the rejoinder of those who "are ready to say I speak it for my own credit" (Rowlandson 61) and responds as a witness—not as the sole agent of her experience: "but I speak it in the presence of God, and to His Glory" (Rowlandson 61). She embraces her responsibility to a higher power in order to avoid those who would potentially accuse her; but, she claims her own personal sufferings and confessions. Likewise, Eliza fears secondary wounding, too; in her last letter entreats her friends to "bury my crimes in the grave with me, and to preserve the remembrance of my former virtues" (Foster 156). Eliza witnesses and endures her own demise but pleads that her friends not think and think ill of her. Both Eliza's naiveté and readers' realizations that her friends failed her were more than likely just two of the reasons Eliza is endearing to readers.

Both narrative voices acknowledge their status of being *haunted* by their traumatic experiences; in doing so, they challenge the notion that their written confessions exist solely as a means of healing or alleviating guilt—or even erasing their queer identities as survivors. The narrative voices refuse to perfectly integrate back into their community, in the capacity that they occupied before the trauma; in other words, they actively maintain their queer subjectivity. At the conclusion of Rowlandson's narrative, trauma is visible; Rowlandson mentions restlessness many nights while everyone else is asleep: "Oh the wonderful power of God that mine eyes have seen, affording matter enough for my thoughts to run in, and when others are sleeping mine eyes are weeping" (Rowlandson 65). Here, Rowlandson attempts to convey the tremendousness of her experiences; she not only has the memories of affect—but also the memories of *visuals* that she yearns but is ultimately unable to completely articulate. The extremity of experience is something that she claims that she has witnessed: "I have seen the extreme vanity of this world; one hour I have been in health and wealth, wanting nothing; but the next hour in sickness, and wounds, and death, having nothing but sorrow and affliction" (Rowlandson 65). The exposure to such "extreme vanity of this world" (Rowlandson 65) has left Rowlandson with the power of knowledge that she wanted in order to prove herself spiritually worthy: "Before I knew what affliction meant I was ready sometimes to wish for it…Affliction I wanted, and Affliction I had, full measure, (I thought) pressed down and running over" (65). Rowlandson does not wish for affliction but rather strives to calm herself against the anxieties of "present and smaller troubles" (Rowlandson 65) by remembering the horror of what she has witnessed and experienced as a captive; but, she is ultimately unable to forget or contain her experiences and memories. She cannot return to her former life unaffected; rather her memories and the residue of her experiences haunt her. Rowlandson's text, in the end, neither dwells on the power of healing nor finding a justifiable cause for her experiences. Like Rowlandson, the main protagonist in *The Coquette* experiences insomnia. Eliza's movement in the middle of the night is often attributed to her consensual and enjoyable sexual liaisons with her seducer, Major Sanford. Yet, I would argue that Eliza is bemoaning her tragic state—whether or whether not she is in the company of Major Sanford—during the night, wrestling her from any kind of peaceful sleep. And, what if Eliza did have consensual sex after Sanford raped her? Does that negate the violence? No, rather, I believe it would further support the theory that domesticity, captivity, and trauma are intrinsically interwoven. The readiness of critics to ascertain Eliza is having—and, more importantly, *enjoying*—sexual relations with Major Sanford points to the larger quest to legitimize or recognize (heterosexual) female sexuality. Indeed, the interpretation that Eliza waits for darkness in order to succumb to her physical desire ignores two of Eliza's pivotal desires, specifically to remove herself from Sanford and to create (and retreat) to a homosocial network of women.

In closing, Rowlandson's and Foster's texts were—and should continue to be—considered queer; these texts created the basis for a counter-public that would only continue to grow and appreciate confessions of trauma. These texts were vital in creating origin points for contemporary memoirs; and they provide valuable ways for us to begin to discuss domestic violence, particularly the ambivalent relationship between abused (captive) and abuser (captor). In applying the discourse of trauma retrospectively, problems may be encountered; but, I think that several texts—like Rowlandson's and Foster's—that have been overly categorized in genre and purpose are untapped sources for both trauma and queer studies. Overall, I am suggesting that early American women writers like Rowlandson and Foster braved censorship and public disdain to publish their personal confessions; and, to become effective witnesses of trauma and survivors' agency, we must learn how to recognize the interaction between written words, the act of confession, and even silences. Contemporary confessional writings are more comfortable discussing sexual topics than either Rowlandson or Foster, but the techniques for describing a domestic or familiar space as a place of violent contention and queer identity continues to be incorporated. In fact, transsexual autobiographies—like Christine Jorgenson's—explicitly adopt the discourse of captivity to explain the trauma of being "trapped in the wrong body." In a post-modern society, we likely find ourselves dismissing Rowlandson's biblical quotes; but, confessions of trauma, especially, challenge our witnessing skills. American women writers have adapted Rowlandson's strategy of using intertextuality in order to reclaim their narratives and speak as an agent, even with the very discourse that attempts to deprive them of that agency; this will be further discussed in the next chapter. We must never forget that it is difficult and sometimes almost impossible to discuss trauma. Survivors use a variety of different ways to communicate their pain. Referencing the supernatural has resurfaced in our culture as a method of communicating ineffable trauma; and, this will be further explored in the last chapter. Indeed, examining Rowlandson's and Foster's texts more closely can help us to really appreciate the boundaries that others face in confessing and publishing their traumas for others to appreciate.

Notes

[1] *The Tenth Muse Lately sprung up in America* by Anne Bradstreet was first published in 1650 in England; it was not published in the Americas until 1678, four years after Bradstreet's death.

[2] This epitaph is used as it was in the 17th through 19th centuries.

[3] *Charlotte Temple* was first printed in England in 1791 but had little success in procuring a large readership. The best-selling popularity of the novel in America attests to the differences in social climate between England and America.

[4] As noted in the introduction, "trauma" originates largely in response to diagnosing the psychological effects of Vietnam veterans, who are mostly men.

[5] See Derounian-Stodola, "Introduction" 55-7.

[6] See Davidson (111) for a comparison between William Brown's *The Power of Sympathy* and Foster's *The Coquette*. Also consult Marion Rust, who argues that Charlotte Temple's (in Susanna Rowson's *Charlotte Temple*) fault is not her desire—but lack thereof (illustrated by the fact that Charlotte collapses at every critical juncture in the narrative.

[7] See, especially Davidson 12-13.

[8] One of the most prominent examples that Tompkins (especially pages 122-146) uses is Harriet Beecher Stowe's *Uncle Tom's Cabin*, which Tompkins argues uses sentimentality to accomplish her political agenda. Sentimentality, she argues is associated with the private sphere, which "is anything but domestic, in the sense of being limited to purely personal concerns" (146).

[9] I use "canon" to denote pieces of literature that are generally considered 'classics', such as Nathanial Hawthorne's *The Scarlett Letter*.

[10] Anne Hutchinson was excommunicated and forced to leave the Massachusetts Bay Colony when she was pregnant with her fifteenth child; and, in 1964, all but one of her daughters were killed in an Indian raid. One could argue, then, her excommunication was a death-sentence—or, at very least, a burden by limiting access to resources that were available by virtue of a larger community.

[11] For discussions concerning the readership and growing middle class, see Davidson (38-45) and Evans (41-3).

[12] Critics such as Jane Tompkins and Cathy Davidson concur that readers emotionally responded to sentimental literature because it mirrored their own experiences—or experiences of those whom they knew. Evidence, such as mass amounts of tattered copies of texts and even the creation of physical gravesites for fictional heroines, attest to this.

[13] For more information regarding Herman's methodology and impact on trauma studies, see my Introduction.

[14] I believe that any experience of trauma will not be solitary; rather, I believe that one *lives with* trauma. Memories of the initial traumatic experiences and even reactions of others' responses to confessions of trauma comprise continually fresh reference points of pain. This refusal to believe that "recovery" or "restoration" equates to forgetfulness or erasure of pain is evident in the latter portion of this chapter and elsewhere in this project.

[15] See Cvetkovich 15-17.

[16] See Rowlandson 61.

[17] See Rowlandson 43.

[18] Most scholarship as well as captivity narratives attest to the lack of sexual violence encountered when held hostage by Native Americans. For a discussion on how Native Americans and Europeans viewed the possibility of owning or stealing another's sexuality, see John D'Emilio's and Estelle B. Freedman's *Intimate Matters: A History of Sexuality in America* (especially pages 8-10).

Chapter 3: Queering the Case Study: Christine Jorgensen's *Autobiography* and Susanna Kaysen's *Girl, Interrupted*

I'm just a girl, living in captivity

Your rule of thumb

Makes me worry some

--"Just a Girl", No Doubt

No Doubt's song "I'm Just a Girl" was released in 1995 and is still one of Gwen Stefani's memorable hits. The song is a scathing feminist, tongue-and-cheek response to gender normalizations. The song begins with the demand to "Take this pink ribbon off my eyes" because she's "had it up to here" with all the assumptions—like mental and physical inferiority—of being "just a girl." This song does not criticize *being* a female, but it does criticize the construction of femininity that renders women incapable of so much—because they are "just a girl." This song drastically contrasts earlier songs like "I Enjoy Being a Girl" in Richard Rodgers' and Oscar Hammerstein's *The Flower Drum Song* (1961), which is later sung by Peggy Lee and Doris Day, where the prototype of femininity equates to being delightfully and constantly overwhelmed: "When men say I'm sweet as candy…It goes to my head like brandy." These constructions feel confining, and as Gwen Stefani sings, like "living in captivity." Struggling with pink bows and dresses seems to pale in comparison to Rowlandson's experience of burying her children and struggling to survive in the wilderness; however, the magnitude of difference in the level of importance is something I want to highlight. Normalizations of gender are not limited to color schemes. Not conforming to gendered behaviors can result in verbal harassment and physical violence from on-lookers by doing something as simple as walking down the street; normalizations of gender have also been cemented with legal repercussions, including incarceration within jails or mental institutions—and should make us all "worry some" (No Doubt).

The physical captivity that Rowlandson experiences and the rhetorical captivity evident in *The Coquette* culminate in Christine Jorgensen's *Autobiography* and Susanna Kaysen's *Girl, Interrupted*. An unhappy George Jorgensen felt trapped in her[1] body all of her life; in 1952, the ex-GI returned to the United States as Christine, capturing the hearts and imaginations of the American public. Her cult status and theatrical performances made her a house-hold name—and icon; and in the 1970s, when she published her autobiography, it was celebrated by medical communities, queer counter-publics, and the general public. Susanna Kaysen, a teenager in the 1960s, also felt trapped—by the expectations of her high-class parents to attend college and act like a demure housewife. After committing herself to a two-year stint at a private institution, Kaysen emerges older, wiser—and with a mental diagnosis that both haunts and perplexes her. Kaysen's memoir gained so much mass popularity that it provided the basis for a film adaptation in 1999 with Winona Ryder and Angelina Jolie, who won an Academy Award for her performance. Like Rowlandson, Jorgensen's and Kaysen's captivities are physical: Jorgensen, by her own material body; and, Kaysen, within the walls of a mental institution and the psychoneuroletpic drugs that she is forced to take. But, like the heroine in *The Coquette*, Jorgensen and Kaysen are also held captive rhetorically—and their captivities are maintained—by normalizations of gender, sex, and sexuality. This captivity is evident by medical diagnoses, alterations to/confinement of the material body; and their rhetorical captivity is evident by their inability to destroy discursive captivity, even after they have been "released" by medical experts as "cured." The rhetorical captivity of gender normalizations becomes evident only within their narratives. Jorgensen and Kaysen resist their "case studies", completed by medical "experts", by writing their own account. Jorgensen and Kaysen reclaim medical discourse in order to interrogate their diagnoses; in other words, they engage the documents and discourse that try to silence them—and many others like them.

Anne Cvetkovich writes, "Even though [Judith] Butler doesn't name it as such, the normalization of sex and gender identities can be seen as a form of insidious trauma, which is effective precisely because it often leaves no sign of a problem" (46). As a result of this "normalization of sex and gender identities," (Cvetkovich 46), both Jorgensen and Kaysen felt trapped within themselves and by others' view of them. At almost twenty years old, they chose the only recognizable solution for themselves: for Jorgensen, it was a sex-reassignment surgery; and, for Kaysen, it was committing herself to a mental institution. Placing Jorgensen's and Kaysen's memoirs in dialogue with each other elucidates how normalizations of gender and sexuality can result in trauma; the narratives—with different levels of explicitness—reveal how medical discourse can keep a material body rhetorically and physically captive. The power of "scientific truth" creates medical diagnoses—written theories—that are capable of binding a body to a specific location (such as a hospital or asylum) and validating actions to that body that would be considered "torture" elsewhere, but are considered "treatment" because they are governed by medical discourse. This is not to argue that medical discourse is inherently evil or inhumane; while it does provide us with the language to make some experiences of pain visible to the masses, its power must be harnessed to validate agency—as Jorgensen and Kaysen both discursively argue. In this way, privileging the confessor's identity is vital in witnessing confessions—especially those cloaked and/or coerced within scientific discourse. Moreover, placing the texts in dialogue with each other also accomplishes other goals of American women's confessional writing, including: privileging identity and agency and rendering discursive (in this case, scientific and gender) trauma visible.

"I Got to Know Who I am"

In the 1950s film *East of Eden*, based on the novel by John Steinbeck, the prodigal son Cal (played by heart-throb and rebel James Dean) cries: "I got to know who I am. I got to know who I'm like. I got to know..." Cal's overwhelming desire to know his origins—specifically about his mother, who could live no better by "the rules" than Cal and lives (literally) on the fringes of town—cannot be contained, even at the expense of hurting his angelic brother's sensibilities or ruining any chance of the paternal approval that he so desperately seeks. While Jorgensen and Kaysen are aware of their lineages, they still struggle on a similar quest for authenticity—with the same fervor that Cal does. Before Jorgensen's physical transformation or Kaysen's institutionalization, Jorgensen and Kaysen lived outside the normalizations of gender. Jorgensen, as a young man, was viewed as feminine—even by his family; his masculinity was further questioned when he could not secure a combat position in the Army during World War II, instead regulated to the feminine task of writing reports. Kaysen refused to be the quintessential debutant that her elite family members wished her to be; she dated her professors, refused to go to college or marry, and ran away from home. What might be termed simple rebelliousness or difference on the surface now, though, was considered a threat to national security and individual psychological wellbeing during the 1950s and 1960s. To appreciate the liminal position that Jorgensen and Kaysen initially found themselves in and how they responded, we must analyze how normalization of gender and the emergence of identity politics interacted within a discourse of ultimate protection—national security.

In *Rebels: Youth and the Cold War Origins of Identity*, Leerom Medovoi argues that the concept of "identity" as we now understand it—as a struggle toward subjectivity—occurred amidst the Cold War "agency panic" (21). There were two responses to this panic: containment and rebellion— and they often overlapped. Both were constructed as superior and identity- building. Discourses of containment largely revolved around national identity, separate from 'the foreign'; and, discourses of individuality, emerging self-awareness—even within groups—was utilized by both consumer culture and civil rights movements. During Cold War America, the term "identity" transformed from an objective description to one of personal and political struggle. Individual and national identities rhetorically overlapped. The fear of internal threats reached an epic proportions during Senator McCarthy's witch-hunts, during which McCarthy proposed that he could contain these threats; Alan Nadel argues that one "...aspect of containment...has come to be known as McCarthyism, a term that describes generically the growing fear of subversion and the extreme measures to counter it, that developed and heightened from the end of

World War II to the early 1950s" (71). One of these "subversions" that Nadel mentions were often isolated in the representative body of "the communist" or communist-sympathizer, who could easily "pass" as American. The job, then, of every "true" American was to seek out anyone who appeared to deviate from the 'American pattern'; those who deviated from normalizations of gender and sexuality became easy targets—not only were they thought to debilitate the moral fibers of America, now they were issues of national security. After the cold war, the culturally acceptable way of asserting one's self was through capitalism—such as purchasing items that personalized a home. In his study that chronicles the evolution of psychology with personal and public identity, Phillip Cushman asserts that this burgeoning obsession with consumerism emerged as a method to focus the post-war emphasis on individuality and freedom: "The partnership between unbridled consumption and the promise of individual salvation, facilitated by the American ideology of inner liberation, has become known as consumerism" (211).[2]

This is the political climate in which Jorgensen's sex-reassignment and public performances began to take place. Jorgensen was forced to rhetorically navigate discourses of gender normalizations—and how they impacted her identity and national security. Jorgensen's hormonal and surgical treatments occurred in Denmark—not the United States. George Stürup, a Danish psychiatrist, once exclaimed to Jorgensen that American's preoccupations with sex were ridiculous:

> "You Americans are so childish about sex!" he said. "'Operate on the brain, perform a lobotomy, create a whole new personality—but

operate on a testicle and everybody explodes!'" (qtd. in Christine
Jorgensen's *Autobiography* 102).

Normalizations of gender were more important than ever, though, in post-
war America. With the return home of GIs and the inauguration of
corporate America, masculinity was being redefined. David remarks, "It
was as if, by way of her conversion from agile manhood to fragile
womanhood, Jorgensen stood symbolically for the vulnerable American
male body besieged by a foreign power" (146). Returning from abroad and
battle, white, middle-class men were forced into clean and orderly offices
while white, middle-class women returned to the home—from the bustle of
factory work. To make this redefinition of masculinity massively effective,
the existence of any ambiguities of gender had to be eliminated—and any
deviance had to be decisively confronted. American doctors and surgeons
refusal to perform sex reassignment surgery on those seeking it, coupled
with Jorgensen's high-profile case, encouraged many others like her to
make the difficult and expensive trip to Denmark in search of help. So,
individuals seeking sex re-assignment surgery became refugees. In fact,
so many persons sought medical assistance in Denmark that the country
placed a restriction on other national visitors seeking sex change
operations. One Danish physician is reported as saying, "There is nothing
Danish doctors can do that cannot be done by our skilled colleagues in any
country. It is unfortunate that Denmark has become known as a haven for
these people and their sex complications" ("Denmark Intends to Ban
Americans in Search of Sex Operations"). Less than two years after
Jorgensen's sex change became public knowledge, a similar case was
reported; the headline of *The Washington Post* article reads, "Second Ex-

GI Becomes 'Woman' in Denmark; First Surgery on Kitchen Table at Midnight." The American medical field's hesitancy to begin "sex changes" on its citizens became a rhetorical response to the supposed inadequacy of other countries' attempts; in a major way, hormonal and surgical treatments became markers of technological progress and superiority.[3] Although her surgeries were conducted outside of the United States, Jorgensen was always eager to strategically present herself as unequivocally American. Responding to a reporter about her happiness to be home, Jorgensen replies, "What American woman wouldn't be" ("Christine Back in U.S. Wearing Mink"). Clearly, Jorgensen wants to be 'read' as a woman—and, more distinctly, part of the cohesive American narrative; the other option would be to be read as artifice, phony—and un-American.

Kaysen's situation, however, is different in that she embraces her status as a visible rebel. The civil rights "movements" were growing in momentum and comprised of particular individuals who formed a coalition to assert their independence and individuality from an unsympathetic (or un-witnessing) nation. According to Medovio, civil rights movements combined the rhetoric of identity and young rebel to assert their "emergent identity, a young self establishing its sovereignty against the forces of a racist, patriarchal, or homophobic 'parent culture'" (3); in this way, the desire and political strategy to conceive of one's self as an evolving dissenter has become embedded within the rhetoric of "identity politics" and even the concept of adolescence. In the 1960s, Kaysen was a typical upper-class teenager. So, typical, in fact, that she jokingly calls her institutionalization "the great Cambridge sociology experiment" (Kaysen qtd. in Beam 198). Alex Beam, who's *Gracefully Insane* chronicles the history of McLean, calls it the "McLean youth experiment" and explains why:

> The McLean youth movement was a response to what an economist might call a market opportunity. Psychiatry was a booming filed, flush with confidence in its therapeutic powers. Doctors were pouring out of the medical schools and were looking for patients to analyze. Many insurance companies were paying up to six months of inpatient care, and the field of adolescent psychiatry was burgeoning. And there was no shortage of troubled young people. The 1960s need no introduction here: Drugs, rebelliousness, and rejection of parental authority were the order of the day, especially in the socioeconomic strata that had access to psychiatric care. (In her official history of the hospital, Silvia Sutton remarks that "delinquent adolescents from less-advantaged homes had other destines, such as reform school.") Conveniently, doctors developed a catchall diagnosis for their teenage clientele: "adolescent turmoil." These were people who probably wouldn't be considered severe enough to be hospitalized now," says Dr. Michael Sperber, who worked on South Belknap and Bowditch [at McLean] during the 1960s. (198)

In her memoir, Kaysen acknowledges her feelings of captivity that result from normalizations of gender, which are affected by race and class (as her father's expectations and annoyances demonstrate). Her upper-class family and, no doubt, her peers thought her odd because she had no immediate desire to attend college or become married—instead, choosing to have open sexual relations. In order to affirm herself, she consciously chose to actively rebel. Kaysen confesses, "I had to admit, though, that I knew I wasn't mad [but...] All my integrity seemed to lie in saying No. So the opportunity to e incarcerated was just too good to resist. It was the very big No—the biggest No this side of suicide" (42).

Curiously, the discourse of adolescence was used not only to discuss identity as emergent (as previously discussed), but it was also used as a means to articulate mental illness; Freud writes, "When, therefore, any one has become a gross and manifest pervert, it would be more correct to say that he has remained one, for he exhibits a certain stage of inhibited development" (43). Thus, Freud's idea of repressed development helped to situate anyone who deviated from normalizations, especially of gender and sexuality, as both socially deviant and mentally disturbed. Medical discourse portrayed Jorgensen and Kaysen as unstable and lacking a coherent view of self and identity—a similar portrayal of how trauma survivors are depicted as fragmented versions of themselves—in order to justify its own legitimacy. Medical discourse, particularly psychology, purports to "heal" these fractions of self; however, while diagnosis seemingly provided the "truth" of the self that was inaccessible to the subject, it also became an integral (if not all-consuming) part of one's identity. The term "transsexual" was coined in 1949 by Dr. D.C. Caudwell; however, German-born, United States citizen, Harry Benjamin made it famous in his 1966 book *The Transsexual Phenomenon*. Transsexuality was often defined in terms of transvestism, donning the attire of the opposite sex—choices ascribed to gender; in *The Transsexual Phenomenon*, Benjamin defines transsexuality and transvestism as "symptoms or syndromes of the same underlying psychopathological condition, that of a sex or gender role disorientation and indecision. Transvestism is the minor though more frequent, transsexualism is the

74

much more serious although rarer disorder" (25-6). But, Jorgensen, at no time, displays "disorientation and indecision" about what she desires; rather, she understands what she wants—and what it may cost. Jorgensen never waivers in her desire to change her sex and gender: "I was willing to undergo any risk, that I would rather be a guinea pig in a case that failed than not try at all, to continue living as I had been" (*Autobiography* 102). Jorgensen's inability "to continue living as I had been" (*Autobiography* 102) demonstrates that she was enduring torture in her physical form; but, nowhere does she seem "indecisive." Likewise, Kaysen demonstrates a high-level of self-awareness—a more keen (although different) understanding than those around her:

> My self-image was not unstable. I saw myself, quite correctly, as unfit for the educational and social systems. But my parents and teachers did not share my self-image. Their image of me was unstable, since it was out of kilter with reality and based on their needs and wishes. They did not put much value on my capacities, which were admittedly few, but genuine. I read everything, I wrote constantly, and I had boyfriends by the barrelful. (155)

But this discursive positioning of Jorgensen and Kaysen as adolescent and "in need of (paternal) help" justified the reasons for medical—sometimes extreme—involvement and discursive containment.

Confessional Science and the Rhetorical Body

Michel Foucault argues that scientific discursivity began to classify and contain the "truth" of sex in the nineteenth century. Foucault writes, "an improbable thing was then taking shape: a confessional science, a science which relied on the many-sided extortion, and took for its object that was unmentionable but admitted to nonetheless" (64). Envisioning sex as the focal point for "unlimitless dangers" (Foucault 66), it became essential to seek it out, force it into visibility, and medicalize its effects. One of the primary ways in which this "confessional science" operates is through the form of the case study: confessions are extracted (sometimes by force), evaluated, and seemingly recorded for the purpose of other scientists who can appreciate and further evaluate the confessions. In this way, the confessions—personal motivations, descriptions of self and pain—have become mere data, recorded and interpreted by others, not the subject. Confession, as a science, became a ritual that was so entrenched in the production of knowledge and power that the subject lost self-awareness and, arguably, agency, within it. Foucault argues that "the scope of the confession [was altered]; it tended no longer to be concerned with what the subject wished to hide, but with what was hidden from himself" (66). Thus, the subject was no longer considered to even *be aware of her/his sexuality*, which is what she or he wanted to hide or needed to confess; the chief tool of freedom and truth, namely confession, was no longer consciously available to the individual. In addition to agency, access to language is further removed from the confessing subject during this scientific confessional. In the quest to classify and contain sexuality, medical discourse has created a vast language of its own—full of symptoms, diagnostic criteria, and terms that are assumed to be only understood by an "objective expert" and certainly not the patient. Thus, the actual confessional voice of patients has become reduced to a mirage of truth, fleeting through the course of records and medical histories, prompting continual revisions and re-interpretations from "objective" medical experts;

76

and this has helped to render the confessing subject as explicitly incapable to decipher her own confessions—because she is incapable of the "objectivity" and "expertise" required to investigate, explain, and understand the latent ways that her sexuality may have caused potential neurosis.

While medical experts did help Jorgensen to feel less trapped within her body and the staff at McLean did help Kaysen guard against successive suicide attempts, Jorgensen and Kaysen had extremely ambivalent relationships with those who tried to rhetorically protect them while also causing them physical pain. The medical personnel whom Jorgensen and Kaysen remained in contact with during their "treatments" are often described in parental terms. Like Rowlandson, Jorgensen's and Kaysen's struggles are evident within the form of their text as well as ambivalent feelings toward those who seek to keep them rhetorically captive through diagnostic labels. First published in 1967, Jorgensen's memoir shared a remarkable resemblance to Rowlandson's text because her benefactor— Harry Benjamin—introduced the text and lauded Jorgensen. While Mather exalted Rowlandson for her contributions to religious discourse and edification, Benjamin hails Jorgensen's narrative as significant to scientific discourse. Benjamin introduces Jorgensen's autobiography, published over a decade after she made her first debut in America as "Christine", as part of her debt to scientific discourse (and, maybe, to him):

> Jorgensen's account is "long overdue," Benjamin writes, "owed" not only to self, family, and fellow transsexuals but "to science and the medical profession"; "she was *in duty bound* to supplement the technical report made by her Danish physicians…with her own account of the inner and outer events in her still rather young life." In

writing her autobiography, the transsexual returns the favor of
authorization, part of a reciprocity between clinician and subject that
continues to take place through the conventions of autobiographical
narrative. (qtd. in Prosser 126)

Kaysen's narrative does not include a forward, per se; however, throughout
the entire memoir, she inserts portions of her medical file that was created
while at McLean. These photocopies of her medical files highlights the
rhetorical captivity of medical discourse that continually tries to interfere as
Kaysen confesses as a subject to the readers.

Medical case studies, as well as medical discourse, lend themselves
toward objectifying the subject as well as depicting the subjects as childlike.
This infantilization helps validate courses of action that are considered
"treatment" but could be considered "torture" in any other circumstance.
Since transsexuality was first considered to be a medical or biological
'mistake,' doctors and scientists were responsible for attempting to find a
cure. In a 1954 journal article, Harry Benjamin describes transsexuals as
people who "truly [are] the victims of their genetic constitution, step-children
of medical science, often crucified by the ignorance of society and
persecuted by antiquated laws and by legal interpretations that completely
lack in wisdom and realism" ("Transsexualism and Transvestism" 50). In
the previous quote, Benjamin represents doctor and scientists as merciful
adoptive fathers to transsexuals, society's unwanted and abused children;
Benjamin was—and continues to be—considered one of the most
compassionate allies of transsexuals—but his rhetorical strategy, evident
here, reveals his investment in maintaining control and power. The extent
to which Jorgensen relied upon—and was made to feel indebted to—the

medical personnel that she encountered cannot be taken for granted. In the preface to her autobiography, Jorgensen explicitly acknowledges that is "prominently in his [Harry Benjamin's] debt" (*Autobiography* xiv). Even though Benjamin's success—his papers and research—were largely based on Jorgensen's case, Jorgensen denies underplays her participation in Benjamin's findings: "If, indeed, I had made any contribution, it must be admitted that at the time of my transition it was purely an unconscious one. To me, it was a matter of survival" (xiv). While Jorgensen's desperate desire to escape feeling trapped by her body, she willingly relinquishes the importance of her contributions to Benjamin's scientific and cultural recognition. I do not wish to argue that sex-reassignment surgery is torture; but, the entire process in which surgery is legitimized is composed of endless interrogations and interactions with medical staff (who do perform these operations)—and that process often encourages inhumane actions that *should be* considered torture.

Instead of being complacently confined to their diagnoses, Jorgensen and Kaysen engage and interrogate the ability of scientific discourse to produce truth and healing. Like Rowlandson, Jorgensen and Kaysen waited until over a decade after the events they describe in order to write and publish their experiences. This restrospectivity also supports the idea that they are more fully aware of their own identities and choices than someone who evaluated them for a few years. Jorgensen's narrative shows how her own self-awareness is the initiating factor for the changes she undergoes—not the medical diagnosis imposed upon her. Rallying herself to confess her feelings to a physician, Jorgensen writes, "I cautioned myself, for I didn't intend to flee from this moment of revealing confession as I had fled so many other moments in my life" (64). Jorgensen was aware that her declaration held the real possibility of being deemed mentally ill; indeed, the first consulted doctor, along with several referred her to physiatrists, but she remained undaunted. Finally locating doctors who were willing to operate, Jorgensen describes months in which she underwent extensive interviews in which experts attempted to "unearth any particular childhood traumas or emotional aberrations" (*Autobiography* 103) that would explain her desire to change her sex. She encountered the difficult tasks of showing an unwavering need and passion for sex-reassignment surgery without appearing desperate—a sign often looked for as being mentally unstable. Jorgensen fervently claims that her masculine traits were "physical and sexually underdeveloped" (*Autobiography* 29)—thus partially visible to others.

Surrounded by women, Jorgensen posits that as a possible reason she lacked masculine gender qualities—because she did not have adequate education about those normalizations of masculinity. Jorgensen's grandmother, mother, and sister seem to influence her childhood the most; Grandmother Jorgensen is represented as the wise, strong matriarch, but Jorgensen's relationships with her sister and mother are fraught with ambiguities. Jorgensen describes her mother's possible parenting flaw in requiring Dolly, Jorgensen's older sister, to integrate Jorgensen into all after-school activities: "How much these girlish activities were to contribute to my future problems and the inability to identify myself with the masculine sex, I don't think I will ever know" (*Autobiography* 5). Here, Jorgensen does not designate one reason as to why she cannot conform to a gender identity that corresponds with her male body; rather, she implicitly challenges medical discourse's ability to find a sole reason, too.

Likewise, Kaysen (before being institutionalized and afterward, when writing her memoir) believes that she has a high level of self-awareness and self-understanding: "My self-image was not unstable. I saw myself, quite correctly" (155). Thus, the problem lies not in the way Jorgensen and Kaysen see themselves, but in the ways others do; this is quite a rhetorical reversal from authoritarian medical discourse where the subject is the one who should be "treated", not the general population's expectations. Like Jorgensen, Kaysen does not explicitly blame her parents for her hospitalization; however, she criticizes their refusal to acknowledge their own delusions by saying, "Often an entire family is crazy, but since an entire family can't go into the hospital, one person is designated as crazy and goes inside. Then depending on how the rest of the family is feeling, that person is kept inside or snatched out, to prove something about the family's mental health" (95). Kaysen undoubtedly seems insensible to her father, who is respected Princeton professor, when she refuses to attend college, enjoys sexual affairs, and attempts suicide. Barbara Schwartz, Kaysen's social worker, describes Kaysen's father's personal (and perhaps professional) reasons for wanting his daughter institutionalized:

> Her father had wanted her hospitalized because she was a stubborn child. She didn't want to go to college. That was anathema to him. He couldn't tolerate that. After all, he was at the Institute for Advanced Studies at Princeton. So there must be something wrong with her head for her not to want to go to college. (qtd. in Beam 203-4)

McLean, a very expensive and prestigious institution, was home to many famous artisans including poets Robert Lowell and Sylvia Plath; so, McLean offered a way for Kaysen to receive "help" and a way for Kaysen's parents to minimize the tarnish to their reputation.

Within her memoir, Kaysen effectively argues that her diagnosis is based on the normalizations of gender—held by society and enforced by psychiatry. In fact, Kaysen argues that the very term of her diagnosis, "Borderline Personality Disorder" (BPD), is evidence of her behaviors being interpreted as on the border between "feminine" and "masculine." In the section "My Diagnosis," Kaysen engages directly with the gender biases of psychiatry, including the criteria of her own diagnosis of Borderline Personality Disorder (BPD). Even one of Kaysen's psychiatrists tell her: "It's [BPD] what they call people whose lifestyles bothers them" (151). In *Through the Looking Glass*, therapist Dana Becker notes that, even after forty years from Kaysen's experiences, BPD is diagnosed more in women—a startling 73.2%. Becker notes that symptoms of BPD include self-mutilation, described as a method of manipulating others for the sake of attention—not as an outward sign of psychological pain.[4] Other symptoms of BPD include "promiscuity" and "on the border between so-called masculine and feminine behavior" (Becker xii). Inside and outside of the asylum, Kaysen's sexuality is presented as particular worry to those who exert control over her: her sexual relations with her boyfriend (inside McLean) and professor (before McLean) are both taboo and reveal the restraints actively placed upon her body and desire. Shockingly, she is deemed "recovered" and released from McLean when she accepts a marriage proposal: "Luckily I got a marriage proposal and they let me out. In 1968, everyone could understand a marriage proposal" (Kaysen 133). By succumbing to others' expectations, Kaysen is then physically freed from captivity at McLean.

Jorgensen and Kaysen portray medical discourse as an ultimately insufficient method of articulating trauma when used to contain individual suffering through medical discourses and practices. Jorgensen strategically does not include discussions of pain from surgeries or uncompassionate doctors; by eliminating those discussions, her pain of being "trapped in the wrong body" remains in the forefront. And, this approach also highlights "the change" of sex as whole and unequivocally positive. Current transsexual autobiographies rely more heavily on explaining the theoretical structures of gender and sex than on discussing the body as feeling and tangible. The lack of information concerning sex-reassignment surgeries and hormonal treatments has prompted activists to include more medical information in their self-help/autobiographical accounts; but, information about how one feels during and after surgeries/hormonal treatments is not discussed—except in the language of "realization of a dream." Bernice L Hausman suggests that "by not representing pain, Jorgensen was able to deflect attention away from the actual surgical techniques that made her transformation into a woman possible; to treat them, in other words, as insignificant to the fact of her present existence as a woman" (356). Therefore, the pain and trauma of medical "technologies" is rendered invisible in favor of accentuating the "realness" of being the desired sex. What becomes frightening is that if the "transsexual narrative" is policed, pain and trauma—as a result and during the 'treatment'—could prevent successive access to medical 'assistance.' The timidity and/or refusal to discuss the pain revolving around the treatments resemble that of selective amnesia, a strategy proposed by most doctors for transsexuals—as well as World War veterans. This relationship between memory, trauma, and authenticity of experience has consumed the discourse of transsexuality and rendered the material body as simply rhetorical.

Like Jorgensen, Kaysen is infantilized in addition to being held captive by medical discourse; she describes the physical space of McLean as "a womb" (Kaysen 122) where "you can't go anywhere" (122). The metaphor of the womb aptly demonstrates the attempt to make the mental institution into a domestic sphere, with its connotations of safety, nourishment, and structure that supposedly replaces the unhealthy home life (particularly with parents) that may have instigated or augmented the original madness. Therefore the asylum is structured to be a 'functional' and isolated familial environment that attempts to submerge patients in an infantile state and thus 'properly' (re)domesticate or (re)habilitate them. Transferred from one domestic sphere (the asylum) to another (the home), Kaysen is thought of to no longer be a threat to herself or others. Throughout her memoir, Kaysen discusses the limited mobility within McLean, including the 'checks' made routinely by nurses to ensure notification of the patients' whereabouts and activities. In addition, drugs were used as a form of control. In *Mad in America*, Robert Whitaker chronicles the treatment of mental illness, citing examples where doctors and nurses used drugs to force patients into infantile states in order to make the patients more 'manageable.' Curiously enough, Nazi doctors used neroleptics, like

Thorazine, during World War II to torture and quiet dissidents and captives. While the Nazi's political motivations and use of neroleptics for mind control were shunned, the use of drugs to perform mind control on the mentally ill are considered "medically sound treatment [that is not] an extraordinary circumstance warranting an unsanctioned intrusion on the integrity of a human being" (Judge Joseph Tauro qtd. in Whitaker 218). Using these neuroleptic drugs like Thorazine and Chlorpromazine has the added benefits of reducing the staff's workload as well as providing the appearance of patient 'recovery'; but, from the patients' points of view, these drugs are seen as a form of punishment and torture. Janet Gotkin, at a 1975 Senate hearing said, "These drugs are used not to heal or help, but to torture and control. It is that simple (qtd. in Whitaker 177). Kaysen comments that the drugs were used solely for the staff: "Once we were on it, it was hard to get off. A bit like heroine, except it was the staff who got addicted to our taking it" (87). Resident nurses would comment that the patient was "doing so well" (87) when medicated with neroleptics; but Kaysen says, "That was because those things [drugs] knocked the heart out of us" (87). Neroleptics have the added benefits, for the staff, of validating the patients' sense of insanity and reliability to their keepers. After an episode of paranoia about being lied to, particularly about her hand containing bones, Kaysen attempts to peel back her skin to see for herself. Following this act, Kaysen is sedated with Thorazine and, for the first and only time, overtly acknowledges that she is indeed mentally ill. Kaysen writes about her relief: "It was comforting [...that] now I was safe, now I was really crazy, and nobody could take me out of there" (104). The sedation of Kaysen's senses finally gives credibility to what others, particularly the medical staff at McLean and her family, have been telling her—her fear is recognized: she is crazy. The relief accompanied by such a revelation may seem perplexing; but Kaysen's is finally provided a cohesive view of her identity as insane and no logical need to fight against it anymore. The actual effects, however, of neuroleptics may have been partially responsible for Kaysen's feelings. Whitaker writes that high doses of Thorazine produce "a chemical lobotomy" (176) along with a feeling of disassociation with one's body, emotions, and surroundings:

> For people so tranquilized, this clamping down on the limbic system often translates into an internal landscape in which they [the patients] feel emotionally cut off from the world. People on neuroleptics complain of feeling like "zombies," their emotions all "wrapped up." In a very real sense, they can no longer emotionally experience themselves. (163)

Earlier in her attendance at McLean, Kaysen writes, "I wasn't convinced that I was crazy, though I feared I was" (159); but after the use of neuroleptics, coupled with being lumped with patients with varying types and degrees of mental illness, Kaysen began to question her initial assessment of her sanity.

Meaning and Truth

Jorgensen and Kaysen explicitly reveal that they are writing for a witnessing public, not a group of doctors, and that their purpose is to promote witnessing—not further objectification of themselves or others like them. Private confessions, the subject of case studies, have long been circulated among doctors—but they have also been available to the general public as sensational material. For instance, Sigmund Freud's published several of his case studies, including one on Dora—who, according to him, suffered from hysteria. From the beginning, Freud defends his decision to publish intimate details of his patient's sexual life; he says that his intention is not to scandalize sex or sexuality, but to benefit medical discourse— which is responsible for codifying the truth and, therefore, healing many. Freud's defense or loyalty to a discourse—scientific, instead of religious—is much Mather's defense of Rowlandson's publication. Freud writes, "But in my opinion the physician has taken upon himself duties not only toward the individual patient but towards science as well; and his duties towards science mean ultimately nothing else than his duties toward the many other patients who are suffering or will some day suffer from the same disorder" (2). And, even though Freud presents his motives as "pure," he admits that other readers may "(revolting though it may seem) choose to read a case history of this kind not as a contribution to the psychopathology of neuroses, but...for their private delectation" (3). In this way, the case study has the hallmarks of a sensational plot—filled with sex and possible penance—like *The Coquette*; but, readers are made explicitly aware that Jorgensen and Kaysen expect them to allot them agency. This is even more evident when discussing the texts with a group and having discussed the impact of the normalizations of gender as setting up their rhetorical captivity (as previously discussed).

Even before writing her memoir, Jorgensen appeared on numerous radio broadcasts and other interviews; her crusade to make her story visible—in her own words—was welcomed by the general public—and seemed to culminate in her written memoir. Waiting to see his daughter for the first time, Jorgensen's father said that he was surprised by receiving hundreds of letters from others who asked for Jorgensen's guidance; Jorgensen's father is quoted as saying, "Perhaps that was why Chris did it this way, to bring the whole business out in the open so those others could be helped, too. There's been so much ignorance and misunderstanding for generations" ("Parents Join Ex-GI, Now a Daughter"). Jorgensen writes about her desire to write as a means to connect to a larger audience— those who attend her shows, wonder about her as a 'person' and not merely a case study:

> What is she really like—personally? It was a question that echoed in my mind. That coupled with the medical contribution of my "case," and the stir of my professional aspirations continued to cause everywhere, led me to review the events and people who had contributed so heavily, post positively and negatively, to my whole existence. For the first time in many years, I labored through the thousands of words printed about me in the newspapers, periodicals, journals, and scandal magazines. I tried to regard it all as objectively as possible, and was made aware again that much of the information about the "Christine Jorgensen case" was confusing, often biased, or made sensational and bizarre by the press. (xvi)

Jorgensen writes that she hopes to create "greater understanding of boys and girls who grow up knowing that they will not fit into the pattern of life that is expected of them; of the men and women who struggle to adjust to sex roles unsuited to them; and the intrepid ones who, like myself, must have drastic steps to remedy what they find intolerable" (xvii).

From the beginning of *Girl, Interrupted*, Kaysen addresses the reader as "you" and begins a candid discussion about her credibility. She acknowledges the difficulty in readers' willingness to believe her over medical experts. In the section "Do You Believe Him or Me", she actively engages the audience members with their dilemma of authenticating the author *or* the clinicians. Kaysen presents documents, challenging the timeframe that the doctor spent diagnosing her—before sending her to McLean. The doctor's records affirm that he spent a couple of hours with her, before institutionalizing her; however, she believes that she spoke with him only twenty minutes. After an elaborate back-and-forth relay of information, Kaysen assess the doctor's interview lasted no more than thirty minutes; and she writes, "I won't quibble over ten minutes. Now you believe me" (72). Unlike doctors, the audience is unable to prescribe treatments or medicines—so what could Jorgensen or Kaysen possibly want from readers? Kaysen's desire to have others witness her trauma and pain propels her to share more with the audience than she may have with doctors—such as her history of self-mutilation. Readers can perform a very significant task that some doctors may be unwilling to do: listen, witness, and not discount or diagnosis pain as way to render invisible. Very late in her memoir, Kaysen confesses wrist-banging and writes, "Nobody knew I was doing. I never told anyone, until now" (152). Her ability to withhold this information from her doctors, as well as readers, reveals both her agency and her power over her experiences (versus the doctors who profess to have authority over the diagnoses and treatment of her maladies). Her confession illuminates her sense of inward torture and alienation: "Part of the point [of wrist-banging] was that nobody knew about my suffering. If people knew and admired—or abominated—me, something important would be lost" (Kaysen 153). In *The Suicidal Mind*, Edwin S. Shneidman asserts that self-mutilation, along with suicidal behaviors, should be recognized by psychiatrists as "psychace [psychological pain which] stems from thwarted or distorted psychological needs" (4). Waiting until the end of the memoir, too, reminds readers who are interrogating the power of psychological healing that Kaysen was—indeed, even if she was not aware of it at the time—suffering before entering McLean. The debate becomes is she better now, a question only she (not her doctors) can answer.

When Jorgensen first returned to the U.S., she founded her reason for needed sex-reassignment surgery in biology (as noted earlier); and news reports about the normality of intersexed (or hermaphroditic, as was termed in the 1950s) persons were rampant. Reporter Alton Blakeslee interviewed doctors at a 1952 medical conference and reported:

> For there are perhaps thousands of Americans living in doubt or ignorance about their true sex...Actually all humans begin life with double sex. Very early before we are born, we become either clearly male or female. But sometimes the mysterious controls over sex go awry. (MI)

Here, Blakeslee both normalizes (and conflates) the intersexed and transsexual conditions while still maintaining a eerie shroud of obscurity that can only be penetrated by medical experts. Jorgensen attempted every discourse that she could think of—she "came out" as a loyal American, a "transsexual," a "child of science"; but all she wanted to be seen as was a *woman* (whatever that is). When the 1950s public found out that Jorgensen had not completed her surgeries (namely had a vagina surgically constructed), they used this information to destroy her credibility and further find fault in her story. For instance, several accounts came forth, noting that Jorgensen was not interssexed, as she had claimed; without biological justification for her transformation, Jorgensen was then thrust out of the closet as an "illegitimate woman—and perhaps more importantly, an illegitimate *man*" (Serlin 158). In 1954, Jorgensen was then forced to "come out of the closet", again, to tell the mass public that she had—indeed—completed all of her surgeries and was a *real* American woman. Several decades later, Jorgensen claim her experiences again through confession—but uses her own vernacular and positionality to assert her agency.

Midway through her autobiography, Jorgensen includes her confessional letter to her parents written in 1952 before seeing them as Christine for the first time. This letter reassures her parents that her chemical and glandular problems have been resolved. She expresses relief at this biological cause because she writes, "I was afraid of a much more horrible illness of the mind" (*Autobiography* 115). She continually reiterates her superior health and happiness that these procedures have afforded her. Jorgensen concludes with a final reassurance, trying to help her parents navigate both the complexities of her identity and transformation:

> I have changed, changed very much, as my photos will show, but I want you to know that I am an extremely happy person and that the real me, not the physical me, has not changed. I am still the same old "Brud." But nature made a mistake, which I have corrected, and I am now your daughter. (*Autobiography* 115)

Serlin writes: Jorgensen's letter, addressed to her parents, in the summer of 1952 "speaks as cultural artifact in its own right, to many of the questions of authenticity and performativity raised by Jorgensen's public displays and announcements" (152). In this way, Jorgensen is "setting the facts straight." This letter re-writes her medical diagnosis as she reclaims her experiences, communicating them with her audience with authority. Serlin writes:

> At first glance, the letter bears an unfaltering resemblance to what is now called, in popular parlance, a 'coming out' letter [but]…was more than simply calculated to mitigate the confusion and anxieties produced presumably by her physical appearance. The letter's goal was to locate and seize the voice of reason and the language of confession: its stylistic conventions, readily expectations, and utterly predictable language would be familiar to any audience, including Jorgensen's parents (152-3)

As Serlin argues, Jorgensen "seize[s] the voice of reason and the language of confession" (153); she does not interrogate medical discourse or respond to skeptics, but asserts her agency—and her authority to describe her identity and body.

Jorgensen conscientiously produces a seamless narrative, one that moves smoothly from past to present and refuses any fragments within her identity; her body, she argues, was "the problem"—and it is "fixed." She uses the pronoun "I" to show a cohesive identity; for instance, she writes, "I am still the same old "Brud" (Jorgensen, Autobiography 115). Seemingly, there is no change from "Brud" to Christine—only a "correction" has been made. However, in Kaysen, she continually refers directly to the reader with her use of "you" (as previously discussed). While her purpose in using "you" may be to foster a relationship to a reader, it may also (simultaneously) illustrate another point. This point is best illustrated when consulting a reporter, John Calpinto, who wrote David Reimer's memoir. In 1967, David Reimer was born in a small town in Canada; but, after a botched circumcision, Reimer's parents agreed with doctors to raise him as a female. As a teenager, Reimer became the trophy that notable sexologist Dr. John Money used to support his theories (which were later discredited) on the power of nurture over nature in relation to gender and sex. Colapinto remarks on David's vacillation between "you" and "I":

> I noticed that when David described events that had occurred prior to his fifteenth birthday [when he lived as a female, dictated by his parents and Money], he tended to drop the pronoun *I* from his speech, replacing it with the distancing *you*—almost as if he were speaking about someone else altogether. Which, in a sense, he was.

In a way, Kaysen's use of "you", then, *could be* an indication of her unconscious effort to distance herself from her memories. Or, it could be a conscientious choice that illustrates the fragmented narrative voice that suffers from trauma. While we remain uncertain as to Kaysen's motivations, the use of pronouns may be an untapped area for the discourse of trauma.

Both Jorgensen's and Kaysen's narratives engage and interrogate medical discourse as a method for articulating one's "inner truth." However, I believe that Jorgensen's narrative is not as explicitly critical of medical discourse precisely because she recognizes that it can afford her—and many others like her—visibility and access to cosmetic surgery. Judith Butler asserts, "The thought of a possible life is only an indulgence for those who already know themselves to be possible. For those who are still looking to become possible, possibility is a necessity" (31); and, indeed, the words that we still use to describe "gender dysphoria" and "transsexualism" originated within scientific discourse. To completely negate medical discourse would be to risk the very possibility of existence. I believe that Jorgensen does not wish to risk this disappearance into oblivion for herself—and the countless others like her who are still struggling to find that possibility of existence. Prosser discusses the influence of her narrative on transsexual identity: "The media coverage of Christine Jorgensen's story in 1952 and her own autobiography in 1967 produced a narrative model for many…for at least it suggested the right projected trajectory" (124). This "narrative map" (124) that Prosser describes becomes pivotal for being recognized by oneself and by doctors as a "transsexual." For instance, Jane Morris, a male-to-female transsexual (MTF), sought out Benjamin after the publication of Jorgensen's autobiography. Dean Spade discusses a critique of the medical field that was popular by the 1980s, but that unfortunately remains accurate today: to acquire any kind of hormonal of surgical assistance from the American medical field, a certain—textbook—standard script is required and "physicians reinforced this demand by rewarding compliance with surgery and punishing honesty with unfavorable evaluation" (Billings and Urban qtd. in Spade 325). The belief that Jorgensen's rhetorical body belonged to science was so pervasive that, one interviewer in 1957 thought her body did, too; the interviewer asked Jorgensen if her phallic "member" was going to be kept in a museum—since it belonged to science (and American legacy), now—and she replied that she was not aware where it was. This is further evidence that the transsexual body is rhetorically held captive within medical discourse. Even in this instance, Jorgensen's penis

94

becomes a phallic representation—not an organ of flesh, blood, and feeling. It becomes a relic—of American science. Bernice L Hausman suggests that "by not representing pain, Jorgensen was able to deflect attention away from the actual surgical techniques that made her transformation into a woman possible; to treat them, in other words, as insignificant to the fact of her present existence as a woman" (356). Therefore, the pain and trauma of medical "technologies" is rendered invisible in favor of accentuating the "realness" of being the desired sex.

Even with the compassion of doctors who were willing to perform sex-reassignment surgery, like Benjamin, the prevailing argument is that a person never "truly" can change one's sex:

> Medically, or rather endocrinologically, we are reminded that no "female" can ever result from the operation but merely a castrated (or mutilated) male, with artificially created sex organs resembling those of a female and, if successfully created, allowing normal penovaginal sex relations. (*Transsexual Phenomenon* 125)

Benjamin's marveling at the determination of male-to-female transsexuals rests on the fact they would prefer to be a "mutilated" man versus a biologically 'incomplete' woman. This sentiment—that transsexuals are little more than performing in 'drag'—was echoed by other doctors, whose guidance the American public was taught to follow: "The patient will be able to move about freely among other persons without anyone suspecting that this is not a normal young woman but a male transvestite whose highest wishes have been fulfilled by the assistance of the medical profession and by society" ("Christine's Doctors Tell of Operations"). The ultimate goal of sex-reassignment surgery, in Benjamin's longer quote above, seems to be heteronormative sexual intercourse; while sexual relations is a specific form of social interaction, the expectation of culturally approved sex cannot be overlooked. Jorgensen distances herself from any indication of mental illness by displaying an unequivocal lack of homosexual desire; in fact, one of the ways that she is convinced that she is indeed transsexual is when she is repulsed by even the mentioning of homosexuality. Jorgensen never was a strict supporter of gay rights; in fact, she attempted to distance herself from homosexuals in her youth. In her autobiography, Jorgensen writes that she realized early in her life (in male form) that she "could never give myself totally to love and affection for another man" (*Autobiography* 33) because of the social ostracism and religious approbations of homosexuality. Indeed, Jorgensen later mentions being propositioned by a gay male and being forced to leave the situation because of a physical reaction of disgust. Conducted a decade before her autobiography was published, an interviewer asks Jorgensen about her thoughts on the "Washington scandal" of dismissing homosexual politicians; Jorgensen responds that the politicians are vulnerable and may place national security in danger—but only because society has stigmatized homosexual behavior, not because homosexuality is innately evil, or "un-American." Interestingly, by arguing that an individual who undergoes sex-reassignment surgery is never truly the sex they are surgically "re-assigned", the individual's sex is still largely undetermined. And, if that is the case, how can any sexual anything but queer (within this logic)? Here, medical discourse's refusal to validate one's identity over normalizations of gender and material bodies is once again evident. The illogical consistencies are important to acknowledge because the framework of science is supposed qualified (and undisputable) truth.

Tropes within transsexual autobiographies and narratives include both a strong avowal for being 'trapped' as well as desirous of change; the intense desire to end the excruciating pain of captivity is reiterated by all transsexuals. As Prosser argues, the trope of "being trapped in the 'wrong' body" continues to be an effective method for a transsexual's body to be 'read' and for the access to medical aid: "As a formula that continues to trope transsexuality in its medical narrative version, being trapped in the wrong body has been the crux of an authenticating transsexual "rhetoric": language, narratives, and figures that the subject deploys to obtain access to hormones and surgery" (69). The feeling of captivity and abhorrence for their body that transsexuals echo (and continue to echo) in their narratives helped clinicians reason that the only humane and logical solution is to provide sex-reassignment surgery. Medical doctor Michael Dillon wrote in his 1946 publication concerning ethics and endocrinology: "Surely, where the mind cannot be made to fit the body, the body should be made to fit, approximately, at any rate to the mind" (qtd. in Prosser 153). To actively deny this quest for authenticity is torturous and cruel. The first recognized transsexual re-assignment occurred in 1922 when a British painter lived only one year with implanted ovaries; this sensational account of someone who was willing to be a 'woman'—even if the event caused death—is embedded within the transsexual narrative. In *How Sex Changed: a History of Transsexuality in the United States*, Joanne Meyerowitz discusses the desperate desire that permeates transsexual narratives. One MTF, seeking Benjamin's help, wrote, "I am *extremely confident* and determined…This drive is [so] fierce and demanding that it frightens me" (qtd. in Meyerowitz 143). Likewise, a male who wished for, but eventually gave up on, a sex-reassignment surgery " 'hated' himself 'for being so overwhelmed by that horrible desire'" (Meyerowitz 142). Jan Morris' 1974 memoir *Conundrum* discusses the internal battle for "truth" as an issue of character—regardless of the potential consequences: "For I was in my early twenties now, and the older I grew, the more abjectly I realized, when I allowed myself the melancholy thought, that I would rather die young than live a long life of falsehood" (46-7). The reliance of meaning to become truth or "real" is paramount to the transsexual condition.

Why Everyone is a Transsexual or Crazy?

While Jorgensen's and Kaysen's texts were both actively embraced by contemporary readers, the authors were also criticized and adapted for public spectacle. Both were the foundation for filmic adaptations, although the film *Girl, Interrupted* earned more acclaim. Various people and institutions refused to witness Jorgensen's and Kaysen's confessions. For instance, Jorgensen's narrative was criticized for being too personal to be thrust in the public realm. Reflecting a popular perception in 1955, a writer in *One Magazine* criticizes the public nature of Jorgensen's confessions: "Mlle. Jorgensen has done a thing, which, in my opinion, every so-called 'intermediate' [sexual deviant, including transvestites and homosexuals] should. The only thing she should not have done is to advertise a very private matter, therefore ruining her chances to lead a satisfactory life in her new role" (28). The verb "advertise" scrutinizes Jorgensen as intending to financially profit from her experiences, an emphasis on her finances that would appear even in her obituaries over thirty years later; but, Americans did purchase newspapers and tickets to nightclubs to watch Jorgensen perform—for decades. Indeed, Serlin observes, "For better or worse, she became a refugee trapped forever in the cultural 'no-man's land' between risqué entertainment and high kitsch" (159). One of the major reasons for this is because Jorgensen's confessions, once adopted as medical "truth", were then lambasted and contained. She, quite frankly, could never come out of the closet *enough* to supplant rigid norms of an expert's version of those norms.

I argue that Kaysen embraces a queer identity precisely because Kaysen does not "answer" 'those' questions of mental illness. While retaining a queer identity, Kaysen allows the reader to witness her experiences in a way that dramatically opposes the medical, objectifying case study. At the end of the quote above, the reviewer mentions something that is continuously addressed: Kaysen's memoir, along with the film, is oftentimes 'normalized', whether reviewers say she is a 'typical teenager' or a 'typical mentally ill patient.' Instead of embracing Kaysen's queer identity, there is a quest to normalize it—make it a 'safe' case study for public consumption. But, in dismissing the queer elements of the text, one denies the chance to actually witness the trauma and pain of the narrative voice. Kaysen, likewise, resists binaries, specifically sanity and insanity. Throughout her memoir, she refuses to admit to being crazy, or not, as well as defining what 'craziness' really is; but, she does critique the ways in which mental illness is determined and diagnosed. Kaysen remarks that "a general taint is useful" (124) because it allows other to feel safe and "normal"; but, she refuses that an absolute, recognizable barrier exists between 'sanity' and 'insanity'—even though espousing her 'sanity' would provide a less murky way to achieve agency over the doctors that held her physically and discursively captive.

In *Read My Lips*, current activist and MTF transsexual Riki Wilchins asks, "What kind of system bids us to make our bodies a problem to be solved, a claim we must defend, or a secret we must publicly confess, again and again" (39). Nowhere is this more evident than in confessional science. Wilchins asks, "Do they never feel a twinge of guilt as their 'studies' merely escalate the politicalization of our bodies, choices, and desires, so that, with each new book, while their audience enjoys the illusion of knowing more about us, we find ourselves more disempowered, dislocated, and exploited than before" (*Read* 22). Wilchins' concern and anger reminds me Jorgensen's keen awareness as a child when she served as the focus of her sister's undergraduate research: "I never read the thesis, but was told I was the subject of it and that she had won considerable acclaim for her work, in analyzing my feminine ways and attributing them partially to the fact that I played with girls so much as a child" (Jorgensen, *Autobiography* 15). This confession of bodies is a method of keeping the body rhetorically captive within the normalizations of gender and medical discourse. This is how trauma becomes an everyday experience—continual unwitnessed, forced confessions; this is how the situations of trauma are perpetuated. There may, however, be a way to afford agency to those who self-identify in ways that are not eagerly recognized by cultural norms or medical discursivity. And, that "way" is witnessing. Butler offers this insight:

> Indeed, it may be that finding meanings is very different from finding truths, and that one way to get to meanings is to suspend the kinds of judgments that might block communication. The confession strikes me as an important moment to consider because not only does it constitute, within the psychoanalytic setting, a communication of what one's desire or deed has been, but the very speaking constitutes

another act, one that within the field of the analytic setting confers a certain reality on the deed, if it is a deed in question, and that also implicates the analyst as listener in the scene of desire. (165)

This act of witnessing is not unilateral; we must also engage our own personal assumptions and prejudices as we listen to others' confessions; in this way, we validate others' agency as well as our own. We must search for *meanings*—what is important—versus the construction of truth that various fields and institutions try to impose.

In post-modern theory, there has been an overwhelming desire to normalize both the transsexual body and mental illness. While this act of normalization can be seen as a method toward visibility and legitimacy, it also potentially denies the specific experiences and self-identifications of individuals. It is important that we recognize confessor's ability to assert their own identity—even if it validates norms. Judith Halberstam aptly argues that "many transsexuals do not want to represent gender artifice; they actually aspire to the real, the natural. Indeed the very condition that has been rejected by the queer theory of gender performance" (50). We need to recognize that behind every rhetorical body, there is a material one. Some individuals use "transsexuality" as a medical concept in order to achieve the results that they need in order to become—and be read as— the kind of woman or man they desire to be. Halberstam advocates that we take the initiative in reclaiming and naming our own experiences and identities:

> Scientific discourses have tended to narrow our ability to imagine sexuality and gender otherwise, and in general the discussions that take place in medical communities about embodiment and desire

> may be way behind those on e-mail list, in support groups, and in sex clubs. Accordingly, we should take over the prerogative of naming our experiences. (53)

Here, Halberstam offers a seemingly easy solution: allow individuals the agency to choose their labels, dispose of them, or simply say that they do not care. And, she also points out that counter-publics are more currently informed and up-to-date than medical discourse; these counter-publics should be fostered at least for the reason that they affirm self-chosen identities. In terms of transsexuality, though, medical discourse is incredibly behind the lived experiences of transsexuals. In *Sex Changes*: *Transgender Politics*, Patrick Califia argues that the rejection of anatomy for sexual pleasure is pivotal for the transsexual narrative:

> The belief in transsexual asexuality also sanitizes the transsexual and serves to raise him or her above the rest of the sex deviants. The assumption that transsexuals, before sex reassignment, aren't having much sex anyway also serves as a rationalization for the often poor results that surgeons get when they try to create functional genitalia to match the sex of preference. (58)

Refusing to acknowledge sexuality in terms of transsexuality is just another way of containing transsexuality within medical discourse, separated from lived experience.

Though Kaysen discusses mental illness with a critical (and queer) eye, she does not dismiss medical policies or advise others; she told one interviewer, "People think I'm a psychology expert, but I'm not," she says. "I'm a writer" (qtd. in Sanchs). Kaysen's quote illustrates her consciousness of performativity in relation to confession; but I would not argue that her narrative becomes completely universal. Andrea Sanchs, reviewer and interviewer for *Time Magazine Online*, claims that:

> She does not answer nearly as many questions as she raises, including the ultimate one of whether she should have been hospitalized at all. Nor does she dwell on the details of her own history. Instead Kaysen concentrates on describing what life in a psychiatric ward is really like. That approach gives Girl, Interrupted its feeling of universality and makes Kaysen seem like Everypatient to a grateful readership.

In Sanch's appraisal, Kaysen's narrative and experiences are so accessible that anyone could have written the text. This kind of rhetoric, though meant as flattery, reduces Kaysen (the person and narrator) to her text—much like McLean's case study does. The film adaptation of *Girl, Interrupted* is another testament to the difficulty of witnessing; like Sanch, the film applauds Kaysen's memoir but ultimately reduces it to an "every (female) teenager." While no one can argue that viewers feel compassionate toward Kaysen, her mental illness is always in the forefront and virtually unchallenged as a stable construct. For instance, the opening scene is her strapped to a gurney, having her stomach pumped after swallowing a bottle of aspirin. And, moreover, Kaysen's recovery is shown as a direct result of her willingness to confess to the staff at McLean—specifically Nurse Valerie (played by Whoopi Goldberg)—and her disassociation with Lisa (played by Angelina Jolie), who revels in her rare psychopathic diagnosis. The division between sanity and insanity is blurred, yes, but "insanity" is shown to not only exist but be curable by medical experts. The film, though troubling the division, renders medical discourse and normalizations victorious in its final message: only a rebellious, spoiled girl would choose not to listen to her psychiatrists—who, though they may be imperfect, still want "the best" for her. Mary Elene Wood warns: "Psychiatry and psychology need to continually be reminded of their own history, of their inheritance of an ideology that first says women are inherently irrational and then proposes to cure them of madness, an ideology that conflates difference with deviance" (170). While Kaysen's memoir accomplishes this "reminder", that is not its sole goal; the memoir is about the confessional voice, reclaiming agency—and then fostering social consciousness. In response to how Kaysen ended up institutionalized, she writes:

> And it is easy to slip into a parallel universe. There are so many of
> them: worlds of the insane, the criminal, the crippled, the dying,
> perhaps of the dead as well. These worlds exist alongside this world
> and resemble it, but are not in it...In the parallel universe the laws of
> physics are suspended....Time, too, is different. It may run in circles,
> flow backward, skip about from now to then. (5-6)

This "parallel universe" is much like Scarry's description of trauma as "making and unmaking the world." Even though the idea of rendering Kaysen as "every patient" or "every teenage girl", we must not forget—as readers—that Kaysen's experience is *her own*.

In 2001, the documentary *Southern Comfort* shows us that archives of living with trauma can exist for witnessing. Directed by Kate Davis, the film archives the last year of a Caucasian southern gentleman's, Robert Eads', life. The camera follows Eads, who is suffering from cancer, and the responses of his loving friends. Viewers feel the gravity of Eads' condition as we find out that he was refused medical treatment—not because of his insurance, race, or legal history; rather, doctors were afraid that he would make their female patients uncomfortable because Eads is a female-to-male transsexual (FTM) who suffers from ovarian cancer.[5] *Southern Comfort* is remarkable because of the amazing individuals who appear on the screen, and also because of how Eads' story is told. As a director, Davis offers us many gifts, including being a witness for all of those who would be unable to ever meet Eads; Lola Cola, Robert's girlfriend says: "the camera became transparent…and as we came to know and trust Kate, her camera faded into the background." I have shown this documentary numerous times, each time having students react both angrily at the medical community and heart-broken for Eads' friends and lover—but, more of the latter. Like photographer and Eads' friend Mariette Pathy Allen writes, "As the film evolved, the medical malfeasance theme became less important than the ongoing essay on the meaning of family and community, sex, love, and intimacy—issues everyone faces" (39). I firmly believe that the film impacts viewers because of Eads' remarkable spirit—but also because the film allows viewers to see him as a person, first and foremost. I firmly believe that my students, few who have knowingly met a transsexual, relate to Eads because they are able to see him in his personal environment as he shares his stories; his life is not presented through a montage of others' reminiscences after his death, a compilation of medical charts that chronicled his deteriorating heath, or an assortment of old childhood footage from someone's basement. No, Kate Davis does not take Eads' agency and give it to doctors, lawyers, or other mediators; she archives Eads' confessions in such a way that cannot be appropriated by everyone—but can be witnessed by anyone. This film, as a text, is a testament to the power and evolution of a tradition that seeks to revolutionize how confessions of trauma are witnessed and archived.

Notes

[1] Throughout this essay, I use the pronoun that reflects the individual's gender identity at the time of this publication.

[2] For a discussion on how post-war America's obsession with consumer culture evolved alongside the emphasis on selfhood and personal identity—and eventually a modern sense of emptiness, see Philip Cushman (especially pages 210-278).

[3] A few American doctors did, of course, begin "treating" persons for "gender indecision"; however, as Jane Meyerowitz chronicles in her history of transsexuality, patients experienced difficulty in finding doctors who would commit and then *perform* sex operations—promises, followed by "cold feet," were predominant experiences patients experienced with many American physicians So, one can understand why Jorgensen esteemed Benjamin and Hamburger, two endocrinologists who remained loyal to their promises. Jorgensen, in fact, chose to pay homage to Hamburger by adopting the feminine form of his first name, Christian, as her own—"Christine."

[4] See Becker 140-142.

[5] This could as easily be the story of an intersexed person.

Chapter 4: Everyday Trauma and Re-imagining the Closet in Alice Walker's
The Color Purple and Laurie Halse Anderson's *Speak*

In *Autobiography of a Face*, Lucy Grealy[1] writes, "Sometimes the briefest
moments capture us, force us to take them in, and demand that we live the
rest of our lives in reference to them" (78). Her face distorted by cancer of
the jaw, Grealy's memoir remarks about more than her face—in a way, the
memoir is about how she experienced life *through* her face. But, Grealy's
assessment that "moments capture us" and "demand that we live the rest
of our lives in reference to them" is an apt description of living with trauma.
Trauma is ordinary, everyday—there are no fireworks that mark it as
obvious. It is not *always* linear or fragmented, as the last chapter
illustrates; but, it is a lens in which the world is viewed by survivors—it
touches everything. Alice Walker's *The Color Purple* and Laurie Halse
Anderson's *Speak* focus on the struggle to confess the everyday qualities
of trauma that they experience. Celie, in *The Color Purple*, endures
repeated physical, emotional, and sexual abuse at the hands of her
pedophilic step-father (whom she believes to be her biological father) until
she is transferred to another abusive man and his children under the guise
of marriage. Mr.__, later identified as "Albert", intensifies his emotional
torture of Celie by intercepting letters between Celie and Celie's beloved
sister, Nettie. And Melinda, in *Speak*, is seemingly happy until attending a
party before entering high school; intoxicated with a few alcoholic
beverages and the attention from an upper-classman, Melinda is separated
from her peers and raped. Her perpetrator holds his hand over Melinda's
mouth, prompting a silence that permeates most of the text. Attempting to
locate help, Melinda calls 9-1-1 but is unable to articulate anything,

including her situation; when everyone—including her friends—learns that she is the one who called the cops, Melinda is treated like a social leper by her peers, teachers, and even parents while enduring daily taunts from her rapist at school. Every semester after I have taught *The Color Purple* and *Speak*, my students have reacted positively. Although they are eager for discussion each discussion, I cannot help but notice the subtly different reactions that my students have after reading the texts. After reading *The Color Purple*, my students are generally quiet and thoughtful; while after reading *Speak*, several students take me aside after the class and thank me for making them read a book that helped them understand how important it is to listen to everyone's confessions. Maybe the difference is because *Speak* is generally taught near the end of the semester; but, somehow I believe there are other reasons, which I will explore in the latter half of this essay.

This chapter explores Alice Walker's *The Color Purple* and Laurie Halse Anderson's *Speak* as texts that belong to a tradition of American women's confessional writing that queers the discourses of confession and trauma. I am arguing that the texts themselves are confessional—not that one portion of the text "reveals" a confession of rape or other abuse. Melinda and Celie engage in written confessions from the beginning of the novels, but these confessions have more to do with the 'everyday' and living with trauma than describing specific catastrophic events in detail. Both texts do not depict trauma as one event that is contained; rather, like an infection, it spreads and affects everyday life. In this way, trauma *becomes* (ironically) ordinary—an everyday occurrence. For instance, every day, Celie battles the diatribes of her husband and his children—and any physical abuse that they direct toward her; but, her experience is not abnormal—they are *normal* for her.   A former good student and out-going girl, Melinda (in *Speak*) becomes the scapegoat for her peers who were arrested—or know someone who was arrested—after the party where she was raped; she is kicked, shoved, and physically abused by her other peers on a daily basis. In *The Color Purple*, "Pa's" physical and sexual violence leaves both psychological and physical marks; for instance, Celie is unable to bear any more children because he "fixed her" (Walker, *Purple* 8), she believes her children (as a result of her rape) were killed by her rapist (the man she believes to be her biological father), and she lives in fear of all men.

There is a strong cultural reluctance to acknowledge the sexuality of children or potential for sexual abuse within marriages; and, yet, this reluctance hides something more atrocious: the refusal to acknowledge the sexual abuse of female children that occurs in the domestic sphere, a place of supposed tranquility, and the sexual abuse that occurs at the hands of spouses. Both protagonists are raped (and Celie, continually) within or near homes—familiar areas. The silence surrounding rape by acquaintances and family members, especially one's spouse, is continually perpetuated by constructions of age and innocence; this silence is visible in *Speak*, particularly when Maya Angelou's books and posters are removed from the local high school. hooks writes, "Children's literature is one of the most crucial sites for feminist education for critical consciousness precisely because beliefs and identities are still being formed" (*Feminism* 23). While hooks does not really differentiate how she is defining children's literature and YA literature, her theories could be said to apply to both; she continues:

Literature that helps inform masses of people, that helps individuals understand feminist thinking and feminist politics, needs to e written in a range of styles and formats. We need work that is especially geared towards youth culture. (*Feminism* 22-3).

The potential subversive power of YA literature becomes evident within hooks' theories. While hooks is looking at the potential for YA literature to be teach young persons about feminism, I think that the same idea applies—and is arguably feminist—to validate the agency and identity of the confessional voice and to promote witnessing.

In *Speak*, Melinda's story encompasses only a year; that year is very intense because she is simply striving to survive as she lives and tries to make sense of living with trauma. Angelou's *I Know Why the Caged Bird Sings* is about more than her rape as a child; but, the memoir is often banned because it includes 'sexual topics' that are 'unfit' for "young audiences." This rhetorical maneuver of reducing Angelou's memoir to a "story of rape" is likened to that of reducing trauma to a diagnosis (like rape). And the majority of Celie's abuse is considered legal—because many legal standards do not acknowledge the possibility of spousal rape. Maya Angelou's *I Know Why the Caged Bird Sings*, however, spans over a couple of decades—including her childhood, adolescence, and womanhood; there are many similarities between how trauma is discursively presented in Angelou's autobiography and *Speak*. Angelou's Mother's boyfriend molests her and threatens her with harming the one person she loves: "If you ever tell anybody what we did, I'll have to kill [your younger brother] Bailey" (74). After these abuses, Angelou "began to feel lonely for" (75) her abuser because her world "for the first time, it included physical contact" (75). After being raped, she says, "I thought I had died" (Angelou 78). Even to her beloved brother, "There was nothing to tell" (79); she rationalizes, "I had sold myself to the Devil and there could be no escape. The only thing I could do was to stop talking" (Angelou 87). When the nurse says that she's fully recovered from the sexual abuse, her family expects her to return to being "the child they knew and accepted" (Angelou 88) who played outdoors. But, instead, Angelou says, "For a while, I was punished for being so uppity that I wouldn't speak; and then came the thrashings, given by any relative who felt himself offended" (88). Angelou also explains the necessity of amnesia, of forgetting her abuse—and the guilt that she felt over the experience: "The intensity with which young people live demands that they 'blank out' as often as possible" (201). Angelou's sense of survivor's guilt, desire not to speak, and lack of witnesses is very similar to Melinda's evolving feelings. What I want to highlight, though, with this comparison is something particular: a survivor's ambiguous feelings toward her abuser. While it is understandable that Angelou and Melinda felt sorry for, or admired (respectively), their attackers, Angelou's short passage above alludes to the complexity of this relationship.

Judith Herman describes domestic abuse in terms of captivity and intricate forms of intimacy: "Captivity, which brings the victim into prolonged contact with the perpetrator, creates a special type of relationship, one of coercive control" (74). Herman continues: "the perpetrator becomes the most powerful person in the life of the victim, and the psychology of the victim is shaped by the actions and beliefs of the perpetrator" (75). While I do not believe that an abuser completely erases the survivor's subjectivity, the *intimate* relationship that exists between a captive and captor cannot be ignored. hooks argues that coercive domination is the most dangerous because it is often presented, and thus masked, by those one trusts as a child:

> Usually it is within the family that we witness coercive domination and learn to accept it, whether it be domination of parent over child, or male over female. Even though family relations may be, and most often are, informed by acceptance of a politic of domination, they are simultaneously relations of care and connection. (*Talking Back* 21)

hooks explains that this situation sends contradictory messages of encouragement and inhibition. And, indeed, Celie and Angelou experience abuse at the hands of someone living with them as family would; and, in Celie's case, it was someone she thought was her father. Like the law's refusal of recognizing spousal rape, the legal discourse also makes it difficult to conceive of incest survivors as possessing agency. Leigh Gilmore notes:

> In nineteenth- and twentieth-century common law, children were defined as property of the father... Incest lies at the nexus of legal definitions of rape and family... She or he cannot withhold it [consent] because she or he does not possess the ability to give it... So, the child does not gain the status of an agent through incest law... (57-8)

Although children are not defined as property, per se, the same kind of rhetoric is still in use. A child, or young adult, is assumed to be under the protection of a guardian—someone who is responsible for her or his wellbeing (and, oddly enough, liable for the young person's actions).

Adolescence and the Concept of Identity

Upon first glance, the similarities between Alice Walker's *The Color Purple* and Laurie Halse Anderson's *Speak* may not be obvious. In fact, one would initially point out that they belong to different genres: most readers would argue that *Speak* is a Young Adult (YA) novel, both about a young person and intended for an audience that is mainly composed of young persons; while *The Color Purple* begins when the protagonist is fourteen years old, the protagonist's maturity to a middle-aged woman and the repeated instances of incest, rape, and emotional abuse—not to mention the text's recognized literary aesthetic—seemingly make the text unfit for young-adult readers to fully understand or appreciate. In Roberta Seelinger Trites' *Disturbing the Universe*, she notes that "a trend has emerged in the way YA novels rely on adolescent protagonists who strive to understand their own power by struggling with the various institutions in their lives. This trend seems to be one of the defining factors of the YA novel" (8). Indeed, Trites discusses how some authors have not intended for their work to be read as adolescent fiction; but, because of their youthful protagonists, the text is often categorized thusly, nonetheless. I want to highlight one of the most prominent ways in which adolescent fiction is categorized. And, perhaps more importantly, I want to draw attention to a text's ability to defy general boundaries between genres within a tradition of women's confessional literature. Ultimately, the protagonists focus on the same goal: acknowledging and appreciating one's struggle toward identity while confessing trauma. To argue that the texts focus on young-adult protagonists is neither quite correct nor incorrect. The texts begin with both protagonists are around fourteen years old, arguably adolescent or preadolescent, by American cultural expectations—and legal specifications. At the age of fourteen, an individual is not considered a legal adult and is legally barred from making decisions that directly impact her or his body. For instance, a fourteen-year-old cannot consent to body modification—such as piercings, tattoos, or cosmetic surgeries. The age of consent for any type of sexual relations, in America, ranges from 16 to 18—depending on the state. But neither Celie nor Melinda defines 'adulthood' in relation to age, sexual experience, or a single event; rather, both texts emphasize the importance of self-awareness and self-appreciation—and as a continual process, not one grand event. Adolescence is marked by the quintessential quest for identity—juggling the desires to conform and rebel; while this quest does not simply end once someone reaches a certain age, the evolution of individual identity is understood in terms of the liminal space that adolescence represents.

The concepts of "adolescence" and "identity politics" have historically evolved together and are rhetorically interwoven. In *Disturbing the Universe: Power and Repression in Adolescent Literature*, Roberta Seelinger Trites traces the concept of adolescence, which gained popularity only after the publication of G. Stanley Hall's *Adolescence* in the twentieth-century.[2] The popularity of the concept prompted mass self-help books geared toward parents of teenagers, social organizations for adolescents, the recognition of Young Adult (YA) Literature as its own genre, and mass marketing of YA fiction to teenagers who were gaining power within the American economy.[3] This cultural embrasure of the concept "adolescence" occurred alongside a transformation of existing lexicon: the term "identity" transformed from an objective description to one of personal and political struggle.[4] In this way, ideas of adolescence and identity have merged within post-war American culture. This desire and political strategy to conceive of one's self as an emergent rebel against authoritarian institutions (like government, religion, etc.) has become embedded within the rhetoric of "identity politics"; the rhetoric of identity and adolescence have become so intertwined within the American imagination that it is virtually impossible to distinguish them. Medovoi writes, "After the 1960s, the narrative of youth, which subtends 'identity politics,' receded from view as identity became principally attached to race, gender, and sexuality" (3). While the discourses of youth, particularly adolescence, in relation to identity may have "receded from view" (Medovoi 3), the connection is still at least implicit.

Like an adolescent, a trauma survivor is in a liminal position and creating an identity against opposition; a survivor struggles to affirm her/his identity while the very discourse of trauma attempts to erase it. First, Celie and Melinda acknowledge and attempt to confess their queer positionality as trauma survivors; the discourse of trauma and other oppressive constructions, such as race and age, strive to erase their subjectivities. The first line of The Color Purple is edited by Celie, reinforcing her own voice's presence, though wavering: I am I have always been a good girl" (Walker, Purple 1). Lauren Berlant argues that "Celie [is] falling through the cracks of a language she can barely use" (837), existing only in negation to discourse and semiotics. Linda Abbandonato argues that Celie attempts "to create a self through language, to break free from the network of class, racial, sexual and gender ideologies to which she is subjugated" (1107). In "Celie's Search for Identity: A Psychoanalytic Developmental Reading of

Alice Walker's *The Color Purple*," Charles Proudfit traces Celie's personal evolution in terms of contemporary psychoanalytic discourse. Proudfit argues that Celie's revision from "I am" to "I have always been" reveals Celie's internal struggle toward self-validation and away from self-blame: "the child victim of rape and incest often blames herself for her trauma; or worse still, believes that this bad thing has happened to her because *she* is bad and therefore deserves it" (17). Likewise, Melinda expresses her struggle toward visibility—just in a different way; like Celie, Melinda remains quiet among other characters. However, Melinda explicitly communicates her queer positionality; this may be because of Melinda's literacy and familiarity with language. While I do not wish to conflate literacy and knowledge, Melinda's socioeconomic and racial status does afford her more opportunities than Celie to become more dexterous with language. Melinda remains silent during her first day of high school, she acknowledges her position: "I am Outcast" (Anderson, *Speak* 2). While Celie and Melinda desire to confess their pain to others, there is a lack of characters willing to serve as witnesses—as the readers can plainly see.

While the characters are threatened to remain silent, simply speaking is not the solution for two reasons: the limited number of willing witnesses within in the text, and the fact that silence does not inherently oppose confession. Both of the texts begin with either the injunction to remain silent or a silent protagonist. After raping her, Celie's stepfather threatens her, "*You better not never tell nobody but God. It'd kill your mammy*" (Walker, *Purple* 1).[5] Not acknowledging her pain—and forbidding her to confess it to anyone—is creating another wound, and deepening the ones that are already present. Pa practically throws Celie into the arms of her husband, with less dignity than someone would treat an animal, with the following warning: "she tell lies" (Walker, *Purple* 8). This perpetuates her desire to become numb to all the violence and loss that is perpetuated by men in her life; she attempts to survive by "feel[ing] nothing at all" (Walker, *Purple* 42). Others contribute to her secondary wounding by not acknowledging her pain and trauma. The church-folk gawk at her, even though "they think I don't notice" (Walker, *Purple* 43); having seen her pregnant twice while she was unmarried—and now taking care of another man's children—undoubtedly caused them to assume that (and treat her as if) she was enjoying her hedonism, versus being a captive. When Melinda is asked questions, she does not offer answers because she writes, "Nobody really wants to hear what you have to say" (Anderson, *Speak* 9). Her ex-best-friend, Rachel, does not attempt to find out why she called the cops, and Melinda cannot bring herself to confess to anyone. Rachel's callousness seems to hurt Melinda the most; she writes, "She [Rachel] doesn't even bother to find out the truth—what kind of friend is that?" (Anderson, *Speak* 21). When Melinda learns that Rachel is dating her abuser, she attempts to save Rachel from the same fate and confesses; but, Rachel accuses her of being a liar. And, her parents and teachers are not any more supportive. Her parents' relationship is dissolving and they use Melinda as a point of contention, each blaming each other for her silence and bad grades; she notes, "I am the victim" (Anderson, *Speak* 35) in some kind of performance that exists for the parents' pleasure. In fact, her parents actively ignore her pain: Melinda's mother, after seeing her daughter's scratched wrist, says: "I don't have time for this" (Anderson, *Speak* 88); and her father jokingly "mentions the need for professional help" (Anderson, *Speak* 74) when Melinda is bleeding profusely from obsessively cutting her lips. At school, she is especially terrorized by one of her teachers, Mr. Neck, who seeks to give her demerits and fail her on virtually any assignment; he tells her, "I knew you were trouble the first time I saw you [...] I can tell what's going on in a kid's head just by looking in their eyes" (Anderson, *Speak* 9). In this way, everyone is inscribing their ideas onto both Celie and Melinda while ignoring—and actively attempting to erase—their pain.

Linda Abbandonato writes: "Celie struggles toward linguistic self-definition. She is an 'invisible woman,' a character traditionally silenced and effaced in fiction" (1106). Abbandonato suggests that *The Color Purple*'s epistolary form "invites us to trace its ancestry all the way to *Clarissa*" (1106). While I agree that Walker's text is a "rewriting of canonical male texts" (Abbandonato 1106), I believe that *The Color Purple* is not simply reacting against masculine traditions of writing but actually invoking a tradition that already exists within American women's writing. British Samuel Richardson's *Clarissa* was published in 1748, forty-nine years prior to the publication of American Hannah Foster's *The Coquette*; and *The Color Purple* bears more resemblances to *Charlotte Temple* than *The Coquette*.[6] For that matter, I would argue that *The Color Purple* also resembles Harriet Anne Jacobs' *Incidents in the Life of a Slave Girl* more than *Clarissa*. In "Philomela Speaks," Martha J. Cutter argues, "The ancient story of Philomela has resonated in the imaginations of women writers for several thousand years" (161). This myth, according to Cutter, "intertwines rape, silencing, and the destruction of feminine subjectivity" (161); but, Walker's text re-imagines Celie, as Philomela, as emerging "way from an existence as a victim in a patriarchal plot toward a linguistic and narratological presence as the author/subject of her own story" (163).

118

Celie addresses her letters to "Dear God," thereby invoking the ritual of confession that relies on "the authority who requires the confession, prescribes and appreciates it, and intervenes in order to judge, punish, forgive, console, and reconcile" (Foucault 61-2). But, Celie is not asking for penance or seeking forgiveness—as the heroines in the majority of seduction novels are; rather, she is searching for a witness. Indirectly addressing the entries to the readers, "Dear God" serves as method for readers to witness Celie's trauma. Cutter argues that the epistolary form lends itself to being a method of archiving: "Celie subversively reconfigures her audience so that an imagined, rather than actual, person is the receiver of the message, and this allows her to shape her message in such a way that it cannot be erased or silenced" (169). I would argue that this "imagined" person belongs to a specific counter-public that exists solely to validate the agency of women who confess trauma. Thus, confession has the distinct purpose of being witnessed. Adrienne Rich asserts, "Feminist history is history charged with meaning. It shows us images we have not seen before, throws new elements into relief" (149). In searching for extraordinary women writers within oppressed groups who share "the astonishing continuity of women's imagination of survival, persisting through the great and little deaths of daily life" (148). In advocating the search for "ordinary" women whose quest was to survive "the great and little deaths of daily life," Rich is implicitly arguing that these empowered women often live *with* trauma—a culmination, most likely, of race, class, gender, and sexuality. Nancy Miller observes, "The arc of becoming through self-knowledge is rooted in but never entirely bound to the stories of our familial past" (543). After finding out that her Pa is not her biological father, but a pedophilic and greedy man, Abbandonato claims, "Celie is

119

rescued from an identity crisis by Shug, who tells her, 'Us each other's people now'; the two women have mothered each other and now elect to be woman-identified women. Implicit here is the escape from patriarchal law" (1111). As stated earlier, Abbandonato argues that Celie's narrative is subversive because it relies on the confessional voice of a woman generally silenced. Abbandonato notes Celie's lesbian relationship with Shug, but she also expands lesbianism as a queer discourse: "the novel is also lesbian in the much broader sense implied by Adrienne Rich's concept of the 'lesbian continuum,' which spans the whole spectrum of women's friendships and sisterly solidarity" (1108). In this way, one could argue that *The Color Purple* is about—as well as showing readers how to—foster a counter-public. Depending on who you ask, this counter-public may be queer, lesbian, humanitarian, African-American, womanist—or any combination.

Although *Speak* is not written in epistolary format, the text is organized by four school year "Periods", which invokes the "removes" within Rowlandson's text and the case study framework that appears in Susanna Kaysen's *Girl, Interrupted*. The text is like a giant 'report card,' which is usually sent home to parents to document a child's academic progress— but sent directly to the reader instead. This form mirrors *The Color Purple*, even if implicitly by seeming like a "report card home to the readers." The last page of each section designates grades for that quarter; but the grades are not only for academic subjects, but also lists social interactions—such as "attitude" and "plays well with others." Melinda's self-given "grades" for social interactions reinforce what the readers are privy to: her thoughts and her turmoil; literally, she is confessing to no one *except* the reader(s) for the majority of the novel—just like Celie in *The Color Purple*.

Re-imagining the Closet

In her landmark work, *Epistemology of the Closet*, Eve Sedgwick posits: "'Closetedness' itself is a performance initiated as such by the speech act of a silence" (3). Both Celie and Melinda embrace their 'closetedness', evident by their verbal silence; but, they do not remain silent—rather, they write about their daily lives as they live with trauma. Silences are "speech act[s]" (Sedgwick *Epistemology* 3) that make the invisible (trauma) visible; by writing to the readers and a witnessing public, the protagonists make their verbal silence, that is invisible to other characters, visible to themselves—and us. The texts do not present confession as the simple opposite of silence; in fact, the texts highlight two types of silences—one that is forced and one that is chosen. Melinda and Celie are both silenced—hands held over their mouths while they are raped; and this act of being silenced, along with cultural silencing of childhood rape and others' refusal to witness their pain, affects the protagonists' choice to remain silent. *Speak* is, of course, titled so because the main character refuses to speak during the majority of the novel—instead, choosing to confess her thoughts to the readers. Continually, her peers and family try to coerce her to speak—to no avail; she chooses silence because she knows that they will not listen. The lack of a witnessing public preempts any desire to share her pain with others. Likewise, Celie remains quiet as she takes abuse from both her stepfather and husband; she thinks that, in so doing, she will be able to survive and wait for Nettie's return, the only witnessing public she is aware of. The choice of both protagonists to remain silent is pivotal because there is a difference between silence and being silenced: the difference is active choice. Coerced confessions are not empowering since they seek to absorb the agency of the confessor; rather, the confessor chooses silence until she is ready to verbally confess—and chooses to whom she will confess. The responses of others, most often, are what circumvent a confessor's desire to confess. In an attempt to render themselves invisible to themselves and others, Melinda and Celie choose silence while processing their emotions and experiences; silence is not simply a signifier of weakness, but the act of *silencing* is a product of oppression and secondary wounding.

Actively silencing someone is, in itself, violent. The originating point of silence becomes evident midway through the book: "I open my mouth to breathe, to scream, and his hand covers it. In my head, my voice is as clear as a bell: "NO I DON'T WANT TO!" (Anderson, *Speak* 135). She gathers up her clothes and leaves the party alone—to arrive home, alone; and, at this point she ceases to feel like a "one-piece talking girl" (Anderson, *Speak* 97). Martha Cutter agrees with "what many recent feminist critics have argued: that rape is more than just an act of physical or sexual violence: it is an attempt to stamp out or destroy a woman's agency" (177). In this way, The Color Purple and Speak both are confessional texts about experiences and individuals that *do not exist*, according to those who have violated them—and all the systems that undercut a woman's agency. While the protagonists refuse to allow their identities or experiences to be erased, they do not simply depict their rapes in graphic detail, laying them out like a spectacle for public enjoyment. Psychological wounds are not always readily visible, which often seems to encourage a survivor's negation of her/his own pain. After accidently falling asleep on a bus, Melinda finds herself at a hospital; she compares her pain with theirs, saying: "There is nothing wrong with me. These are really sick people" (Anderson, *Speak* 113). Melinda describes her disorientation as she tries to reconcile her psychological pain and identity as a trauma survivor; she asks herself, "Did he rape my head, too?" (Anderson, *Speak* 165).

Both Celie and Melinda embrace the performative nature of confession—and, by doing so, queer the ritual of confession itself. Both protagonists are aware of the performativity of identity, which is why they both seek a mixture of private and public spaces—along with silences and confessions. Don Lantham writes: "Melinda's archive is both a public and private one—public in the sense that the art teacher and other students in the class witness the creation of the various works throughout the year, and private in the sense that Melinda takes most of these works into her closet at school as a way of making the space her own and reconstructing her identity" (378). The fact that Melinda uses the closet in "reconstructing her identity" (Lantham 378) is significant. The symbol of 'the closet' is laden with queer associations; someone who is 'in the closet' is generically thought to be hiding her/his queer identity. The negative connotations of the closet can seem to mire the process of confessing one's identities; but, *Speak* offers another view of 'the closet' as we know it. *Speak* offers a portrayal of 'the closet' as a queer space that can help validate one's sense of self before verbally confessing one's identity or trauma. Fleeing the tyrannical Mr. Neck (her Social Studies teacher and P.E. coach), Melinda discovers an abandoned janitor's closet. Here, she can choose to be silent without the pressures of coerced confessions or secondary wounding; she says: "This closet is abandoned—it has no purpose, no name. It is the perfect place for me" (Anderson, *Speak* 26). But, this closet is not a place of mere confinement. In her closet, Melinda finds validation in women's confessional writing, particularly Maya Angelou's work. Significantly, it is in this closet that Melinda also confronts her attacker for the second time. Following her into the closet, Melinda's rapist attempts to attack her again; but, this time: "Maya Angelou looks at me. She tells me to make some noise. I open my mouth and take a deep breath" (Anderson, *Speak* 194). Taking a broken shard from her Maya Angelou poster, she draws upon Angelou's strength to threaten her attacker into silence. Angelou's presence signifies the pivotal need for witnessing; through Angelou's refusal to remain silenced, Melinda is encouraged to break her silence— and shouts "No" to her attacker, attracting witnesses to the scene. The possible positivism of choosing silence is reinforced when Melinda leaves her closet for someone else who may need it; this emphasizes that chosen silence can be a form of resistance—especially if it leads to healing and one does not intend to live there forever.

The comparative "closet" in *The Color Purple* is Shug's bedroom in Mr.__'s house. Like Melinda's closet, the space is located within a highly charged environment; but, the "closet" is devoid of immediate dangers. With Shug, Celie is able to commune with another human being and recognize her own worth and sexuality. Celie does not verbally confess her pain or sexual abuse until half-way through the novel; while the house is devoid of men, Celie and Shug share intimate conversations and physical closeness. Discussing her experiences with her father, Celie is overwhelmed and cries "like it all come back to me" (Walker, *Purple* 112). Reliving her experiences within the arms of the woman she loves, Celie's pain is finally able to be witnessed. Witnessing does not cure the pain and trauma—but, especially in this instance, it does provide something necessary for healing: love. And one could easily argue that Shug's love and witnessing helps Celie to not only leave Mr.__'s house but also to "talk back" to him before doing so. Celie singularly raises her head and speaks: "You a lowdown dog is what's wrong, I say. It's time to leave you and enter into the Creation" (Walker, *Purple* 199). By this, Celie is asserting herself against her attacker and "coming out of the closet"—just like Melinda does. The implications of re-imagining the closet as a potentially liberating space—as long as one moves out of it—accomplishes two important tasks: erases the stigma of 'the closet' and identities associated with it, and also creates the potential for understanding other spaces—such as homes and schools—as confining (not liberating) spaces.

Some critics claim that the meta-narrative of *The Color Purple* involves criticism of slavery; while that might be the case, I think the text actually highlights the subtle difference between slavery and captivity. The strong and proud Sofia in *The Color Purple*, who is forced to be the white mayor's maid, talks with the other women African-American about how she is always "slaving away" (Walker, *Purple* 102), but her son objects to that word. Sophia responds: "They got me in a little storeroom up under the house, hardly bigger than Odessa's porch, and just about as warm in the winter time. I'm at they beck and call all night and all day. They won't let me see my children. They won't let me see no mens. Well, after five years they let me see you once a year. I'm a slave, she say. What would you call it?" (Walker, *Purple* 103). Her young son responds, "A captive" (Walker, *Purple* 103). My goal in differentiating between the two states, captivity and slavery, is not to create a hierarchy of pain or trauma; rather, I think that making this distinction may contribute to discourses on trauma and construction of power. Both captivity and slavery involve confinement and varying degrees of torture, but the means to which this confinement is enforced differs. A captive is *aware* of being kidnapped and has a reason to continually search for an escape route; thus, a captive *may* have the hope of a reunion to familiarity that a slave may not. For instance, both Celie and Melinda long for a reunion with those who signify a happier time in the past: Celie longs to be reunited with her sister; and Melinda, with her ex-best friend. The importance of recognizing captivity within *The Color Purple* helps us to acknowledge the different types of domestic captivity— and how constructions of race and class, and even legal precedents, help to mask its insidious nature.

Celie and Melinda strive through the entire texts to assert their subjectivity; but, they are also trying to do something even more fundamental: survive. Celie justifies her lack passivity toward her abusers: "I don't fight, I stay where I'm told. But I'm alive" (Walker, *Purple* 21). Both texts also contribute to the overall discourse of trauma, including highlighting the difficulty of articulating it and reimagining it as a *lived* experience (versus one stable event). Both protagonists struggle to name their pain, illustrating the inability of language to encompass their experiences of trauma. The word "rape" never appears in *The Color Purple*; yet, it is undeniably present. This is the case in Hannah Foster's *The Coquette* (1797). The word "rape" is used only three times in *Speak*: the first instance is on a television talk show, where Melinda listens to a survivor's account and wonders "Was I raped?" (Anderson, *Speak* 164); until she witnesses another's confession of trauma, she seems unable to relate to the word "rape" to her experiences. Melinda's inability to articulate with certainty that she was raped stems from her inability to mentally process and name her pain—as well as her desire to forget. Similarly to Melinda, the word "rape" seems ominously absent from Celie's vocabulary. Anne Cvetkovich argues that trauma resides not only in a story, but also in concrete items: "The memory of trauma is embedded not just in narrative but in material artifacts, which can range from photographs to objects whose relation to trauma might seem arbitrary but for the fact that they are invested with emotional, and even sentimental value" (7-8). For instance, in an effort to communicate trauma and make it visible, both novels use the images of trees. When raped, both protagonists distance themselves from their bodies by focusing on another living organism: a tree. Significantly, Melinda is raped, outside and under a tree at a party before her freshman year in high school. Continuously, Melinda attempts to "rake the leaves out of my throat" (Anderson, *Speak* 168) but fails; the leaves are actually choking the life out of Melinda, just like the memory of her rape and the continual bullying by her peers after-the-fact. Likewise, Celie, while being beaten by her sexually and physically abusive husband, becomes a tree— silent and still: "It all I can do not to cry. I make myself wood. I say to myself, Celie, you a tree. That's how come I know trees fear man" (Walker, *Purple* 22). The heroines focus so intently on the tree that they *become* the tree—immobile and silent. The tree, then, not only comes to signify the protagonists' trauma—but also the lens by which they see the world.

127

Confessions and Silences

Confession, both written and oral, is a vital part to the heroines' healing process and promoting witnessing. Their confessions are evidence of, not the sole reason for, their growing self-awareness. As Celie and Melinda become more willing to openly acknowledge their agency, they begin to embrace their queer identity as trauma survivors—and eventually embark on healthy relationships with other characters. Melinda's sarcasm toward her teachers, parents, and peers is evident to the readers—while everyone surrounding her is oblivious to her thoughts, precisely because she remains silent. Even so, the reader is aware that the protagonist is not divulging why she is so miserable—and silent to other characters. These confessions to the readers open up a space where the protagonists can eventually confide in those surrounding them. Diligently working in Art class because she finds validation in her artwork and by her teacher, one of Melinda's ex-friends accidently spoils her shirt with markers. This ex-friend, Ivy, apologizes and is sympathetic to Melinda, discussing their ex-friend Rachel's new snobbery. In front of Ivy, Melinda scrawls on the bathroom wall "Guys to Stay Away from" (Anderson, *Speak* 175) and lists her abuser by name. Her anonymous written confession of being violated elicits other anonymous girls' confessions of similar assaults by her rapist; when Ivy points out the support of other girls, Melinda says, "I feel like I can fly" (Anderson, *Speak* 186). The physical "chat room" or "blog" on the walls of the bathroom emphasize the significance of community—and witnessing—for healing. And, choosing a locale that is mostly available to her female peers, Melinda intuitively creates a community based the witnessing of confessional writing. This example reveals how confessional writing—with a level of permanency that verbal confessions often do not have—is critical in the development of a witnessing community. This space also allows Melinda the freedom of not being rejected or secondarily wounded—as she is when she shares her written confession to Rachel, who refuses to believe her. Receiving the validation and support from the bathroom wall is critical in Melinda's ability to continue confessing, in an effort to eventually break her verbal silence to others.

Some critics have attempted to validate the potential subversive nature of Melinda's silence; but, this attempt is usually circumvented, ironically, by *requiring* Melinda's continual silence. Chris McGee claims that Melinda is empowered by her silence; but, when she confesses, she 'gives in' to the pressures to confess and succumbs to the Foucauldian theory that power produces rituals of truth; he writes:

> I see great power in Melinda's silence, her questioning and resistance to power, and her willingness to work through her own traumas in her own way, even though all of this may frustrate readers. For Anderson, however, truth is indeed a thing constantly to be striven for. It is okay not to speak for a little while, Anderson might say, but in the end you should never hide anything from adults. (185)

McGee writes about his students who are aggravated at Melinda's delayed confession of rape; one male student acknowledges his anger at Melinda: "What makes some people so weak that they cannot [speak]? I just don't understand" (qtd. in McGee 184). Having taught *Speak* multiple times, I have heard the same reactions from students. But, I would argue that the point is not *when or if* Melinda discusses her rape; to regulate the importance of the novel to Melinda's confession of rape is a great disservice to the novel's goal of presenting how one lives with trauma—and how trauma affects every aspect of one's life. The novel's focus is not describing the event of a rape, which is evident by two facts: the book delays including the first and only account of it until half-way mark; and the book intentionally preempts another description of it at the end. The book's title highlights the importance of the word "speak"; and, McGee argues that Melinda cleverly avoids Foucault's "incitement to discourse"—until the end. But here is a critical point: we, as readers, *never* see Melinda *verbally* confess to another character about her rape or about her pain; she alludes to her rape when writing on the bathroom wall and writing a note to her friend Rachel. When attempting to rape her for the second time, and in her closet, the perpetrator says, "You're not going to scream. You didn't scream before. You liked it" (Anderson, *Speak* 194). Finally, though, "a sound explodes from me. "NNNOOO!!!" (Anderson, *Speak* 194). Thus, the importance of Melinda "speaking" is to ward off more abuse—not to provide the details of her rape.

Fraught Witnessing and Restoration

Witnessing is an action—one that validates the humanity of the survivor and does not dismiss pain or the reoccurring effects of trauma; but this action can be fraught with ambiguities and missives. Harpo, Albert's eldest child, becomes frustrated with his independent and brawny wife, Sofia; when Harpo asks for advice, Albert tells him to beat his wife into submission. Celie concurs but later regrets encouraging Harpo to assault his wife; she realizes, unable to sleep, that "I sin against Sofia spirit" (Walker, *Purple* 39). Not witnessing Sofia's pain, but rather perpetuating it,

Celie feels ashamed. Sofia refuses to allow Harpo to beat her, fighting him back; and she becomes enraged when she learns that Celie advised Harpo to assault her. Sofia confronts Celie, confessing that "All my life I had to fight. I had to fight my daddy. I had to fight my brothers. I had to fight my cousins and my uncles....but I never thought I'd have to fight in my own house" (Walker, *Purple* 40). While Celie does not confess her pain to Sofia, she witnesses Sofia's confession of trauma—along with the strength embodied in Sofia's struggle and the act of confession, itself. Celie neither dismisses Sofia's confession of trauma nor attempts to overshadow it with her own trauma; rather, Celie confesses her own weakness in perpetuating violence toward women: "I say it cause I'm a fool, I say. I say it cause I'm jealous of you. I say it cause you do what I can't" (Walker, *Purple* 40). Although Celie admits to being unable—at least at that moment—to fight, she confesses that she wishes she possessed that strength; and, though she does not begin fighting Albert, witnessing Sofia's strength and pain encourages her desire to confess her own pain to Shug Avery—and for her eventual departure from her husband's abusive roof. The instance of Sofia's confession of trauma reveals the power of witnessing—and being witnessed. Shortly thereafter, Sofia leaves her husband and the hostile environment; and Celie's pain, though not explicitly confessed to any character yet, surfaces for the reader to witness. This example also reveals the cost of refusing to witness: perpetual violence. Refusing to acknowledge Sofia's pain, and thus attempt to prevent the violence she experiences, Celie enables the patriarchal violence that plagues her life as well; this action contrasts Celie's apology and later witnessing of Sofia's struggle with male violence. Mr.__'s first wife, Julia, is also evidence for how the lack of witnessing perpetuates violence. Julia, aware that her

131

husband was cheating on her with Shug, had no witnessing public: "And she never told nobody. Plus, she didn't have nobody to tell" (Walker, *Purple* 270). This lack of witnesses aids Julia's jealous boyfriend in literally making Julia disappear—by killing her without anyone's interference.

A witnessing public helps to encourage a survivor's healing—but even confessing to such a group is not a "cure." Both Celie and Melinda are in the company of those who have witnessed their struggles—the sympathetic readers and characters. This is a strong departure from stories such as *The Scarlett Letter*, where a social outcast continues to embrace her trauma versus nurturing intimate relationships with the characters in her town—or the readers of the text. Celie and Melinda do not become legends, like the benevolent Hester Prynn or the mythological Daphne, who flees Zeus' sexual demands by transforming into a tree; rather, the characters continue to be very much *real*.

The protagonists embrace their queer identity as someone who lives with trauma; in doing so, they refuse to end their narrative as a "happily ever after," remiss in forgetting pain. Neither text ends in a way that promises complete serenity for the remainder of the characters' lives. The finale presents Celie and her family "celebrating each other" (Walker, *Purple* 287); but they recognize that doing so does not erase pain and oppression. When asked why family reunions are always on the 4th of July, Harpo responds, "White people busy celebrating they independence from England July 4th,...so most black folks don't have to work" (Walker, *Purple* 287). Complete emancipation and freedom from traumas and oppressions have not been achieved, and none of the characters suffer from the delusion that they have. Celie closes the novel with a sense of hope: "And us so happy. Matter of fact, I think this the youngest us ever felt" (Walker, *Purple* 288). In this way, readers are reminded that while vast hope exists for the characters, much work is to be done in order to create a world where celebrations like this are more frequent.

Speak closes as Melinda as she submits her final art project—a drawing of a tree, of how she sees herself in relation to trauma: "It wasn't my fault. He hurt me. It wasn't my fault. And I'm not going to let it kill me. I can grow" (Anderson, *Speak* 198). Her teacher, who has encouraged Melinda to speak all semester, says, "You've been through a lot, haven't you" (Anderson, *Speak* 198). Her words "float up" (Anderson, *Speak* 198), and her act of speaking is overtly visible within the text:

Me: "Let me tell you about it. (Anderson, *Speak* 198)

The ending of the novel does include a graphic account of Melinda's rape— but the tears and resiliency to live and to "grow." By not ending the novels with a graphic confession of pain, the characters refuse to be integrated into a complete restoration narrative; they lay claim to their own narratives by not indulging in the reader's fantasy of a complete confession. Since the novels are about living with trauma—and not about trauma contained within one event—the protagonists' confessions of their rapes are mediated by different mechanisms. For instance, Celie confesses to Shug about her step-father's and Mr.__'s abuse; and, Melinda describes her rape half-way through the novel and through flash-backs.

Berlant argues that Celie is reborn and her trauma is erased after her "ascension to speech" (852); Berlant claims that "she is completely reborn, without bearing witness to the scars left in knowledge and memory" (852). However, Celie's letters and Melinda's art project show that both of the protagonists are conscientiously creating archives for present and future witnesses. The depiction of trees transforms throughout the texts and comes to signify the healing—but not the erasure of trauma. Like Daphne, who flees Zeus by becoming a tree, Celie and Melinda focus on the image of the tree until they almost embody it; their goals are to become numb—in order to survive—since running away is impossible. Celie begins to adopt Shug's view of God as "part of everything" (Walker, *Purple* 195). And, trees—among other elements—become her witnesses; in the last letter, Celie does not write to God or Nettie. She addresses her letter thusly: "Dear God, Dear stars, dear trees, dear sky, dear peoples. Dear Everything. Dear God" (Walker, *Purple* 285). Likewise, trees for Melinda become a way of communicating—of bearing witness to her strength as a character.

Walker and Anderson acknowledge the importance of confession and witnessing in the creation of their characters; but, as a female author, their confessions—even those in their fictional work—are perceived as quintessentially *personal*. Like their main protagonists, the authors also refuse to indulge readers' insatiable desire to hear a confession based on a contained experience of trauma. Anderson shies away from any explicit confessions about how the novel resembles her own life; she says, "A couple of the incidents from *Speak* were taken right out of my life" (Anderson, "Interview" 200). But, those "incidents" that she mentions are comprised of her experience as "the obnoxious kid in English class who grilled my teacher about symbolism and refused to accept her answer"

(Anderson, "Interview" 200). Nowhere does she confess to having been raped or knowing someone who was raped during her high school experience. My students note Anderson's personal evasion of any discussion about trauma, bullying, and rape. While my students are most curious about whether Anderson was confessing for herself, I am more interested in *why* my students felt compelled to know Anderson's personal history. Likewise, Walker refuses to confess that her characters are based on herself. Walker's *In Search of Our Mother's Gardens* discusses her process for writing the novel; she says that "one or more of my characters—Celie, Shug, Albert, Sofia, or Harpo—would come for a visit. We would sit wherever I was sitting, and talk" (*Gardens* 159). The Color *Purple* is dedicated "To the Spirit: without whose assistance/Neither this book/Nor I/Would have been/Written" (front matter). The concluding quote is from Walker, who lists her credentials as author and medium: "I thank everyone in this book for coming" (Walker, *Purple* 289). She, like Anderson, witnesses her heroines and then this allows the readers to become witnesses. But, my students do not seem to be as interested in Walker's shared experiences with Celie as they are with Anderson's with Melinda.

In "The Evolution of Alice Walker", Cynthia Cole Robinson explores how Alice Walker's personal revelations affected her writings by placing Walker's critical writings and fiction in dialogue with each other. Robinson discusses Walker's experiences of growing-up as an African-American woman in the South as instrumental in her writing. Robinson also mentions a scar that Walker received when she was a young girl: one of her elder brothers accidently shot her with a 'BB' gun and the bullet caused permanent blindness in one of her eyes. Robinson posits, "Through her scar, she began to understand and identify with others' scars" (295). I am hesitant to agree with Robinson's logic that trauma is what brings survivors "together" or that suffering begets knowledge and understanding. Walker does, though, say that her then three-year-old daughter's appreciation for her glass eye is pivotal in revising her personal sense of beauty and worth; her daughter, instead of shrinking away from her mother's "difference," says with wonder: "Mommy, there's a world in your eye" (Walker, *Gardens* 370). *In Search of Our Mother's Gardens* is dedicated to Walker's daughter; there, Walker emphasizes this redefinition of self and trauma by saying that her daughter "saw in me/what I considered/ a scar/ And redefined it/as/a world" (*Gardens* viii). I believe that Walker is privileging identity—as an evolutionary process—over trauma and scars; the way in which she views her scar is what has altered—not the erasure of the scar or the memories associated with it.

The Verdict: Then and Now

Walker's canonical text was published in 1982; and, three short years later, it was adapted into a 11-Academy-award-winning film, directed by Stephen Spielberg, and starred a powerful cast—including such celebrities as Oprah Winfrey, Whoopi Goldberg, and Danny Glover. Laurie Halse Anderson's novel *Speak* was published in 1999, over a decade after *The Color Purple*. And *Speak* was adapted for the screen, too, but on a smaller budget; in 2004 *Showtime* distributed the film, which starred Elizabeth Perkins, D.B. Sweeney, and Kristen Stewart (who would later become noted as the teenage heart-throb in the blockbuster *Twilight*). In my opinion, both *The*

Color Purple and *Speak* film adaptations fall short of the novels' witnessing and subversive power. In *The Color Purple*, the love affair between Celie and Shug is too conveniently ignored that it's scandalous. In the novel *Speak*, the 'adults' are presumably the ones who regulate knowledge because of their status of power; but, while these adults generally abuse their power, their awareness and knowledge of the world around them is ultimately revealed to be inferior to the youthful protagonists. In the film version of *Speak*, Melinda confesses to her parents—who are completely absent and dismissal of her pain and presence in the novel; this, in my opinion, tries to soften the implications of the novel's critique.

The novels' and films' popularity was (and continues to be) contrasted with adamant disgust. In 1983, Alice Walker received the Pulitzer Prize for *The Color Purple*; and, in 2009, Anderson received the Margaret A. Edwards Award for her novels, including *Speak*, for "her significant and lasting contribution to writing for teens" (ALA). Both novels are considered, by some, to be dangerous—particularly in the hands of young adults. *The Color Purple* was labeled "smut" in one Pennsylvania school district in 1992; and it continues to be seen by some as unfit reading for youth because of its portrayal of sex, sexuality, profanity, God, and African-American men. ALA's Office for Intellectual Freedom notes that nearly 6,000 young adult books were challenged during the years of 1990-2000; and, *Speak* is listed of one of the most challenged during this timeframe for its references to self-mutilation and rape. In the 1980s, several critics, such as Salim Muwakkil, recognized the negative publicity surrounding Walker as a struggle against emerging Black Feminist politics. Earlier, Walker had published *In Search of Our Mother's Gardens*, in which she distinguishes "womanism" and "feminism"; she argues that "womanism" explicitly recognizes the needs and experiences of African-American women. Walker defines "womanism" as:

> 1) A black feminist of feminist of color [...] 2) A woman who loves other women, sexually and/or nonsexually. Appreciates and prefers women's culture [...] 3) Loves herself. *Regardless.* 4) Womanist is to feminist as purple is to lavender. (*Gardens*
>
> xii)

I agree with Muwakkil and others who argue that censorship of *The Color Purple* is strategic; it is an overt refusal to witness the experiences and trauma of "an 'invisible woman,' a character traditionally silenced and effaced in fiction" (Abbandonato 1106). Celie—as an African-American, lesbian, rape and incest survivor, and quasi-literate woman—portrayed as powerful is disruptive and frightening to white, masculine, heteronormative institutions of power.

One could argue that, with the advent of the cinematic adaptation, the novels have become easier to disparage—merely by virtue that more people have probably seen the films than have read the novels; and, this situation also encourages the conflation of film and novel. The popularity of critiques surrounding the novels and films has become more familiar to many people than the texts, themselves—especially in relation to *The Color Purple*. What remains curious is that many of the most vehement and outspoken protesters of the texts acknowledge the fact that they have not—and do not intend—to read the novel or view the films in entirety. For instance, Courland Milloy, a black male columnist for *The Washington Post*, said: "As far as I'm concerned I don't have to see this movie to write about

138

it" (qtd. in Bebo). Likewise, snippets of text are selected from YA literature, such as *Speak*, when parents attempt to withdraw the books from the library; anyone who reads these snippets are encouraged—and somehow viewed as competent—to assess the novel as a whole. This reveals that the opposition to the texts originates in response to discourses that exist outside of the texts themselves.

When I teach *Speak*, I ask my students—if they do not offer the information themselves—if they were aggravated at the fact that Melinda takes 'so long' to say that she was raped. Many of at least admit to understanding why someone would be aggravated. I think this is an important discussion to have about the novel—and it is one that the novel itself encourages. The frustration directed at survivors of trauma for remaining silent reveals cultural ideas about trauma and silence. Wondering why someone does not "pull herself up by her own bootstraps" and just leave an abusive situation is a more subtle form of blaming the victim—as if the survivor perpetuated and facilitated her own abuse. What is not recognized, however, is the psychological effects of trauma, which strives (itself) to erase one's identity—and, a more taboo topic: the ambivalence that survivors often feel toward their abusers. Students do not, though, ask as often why Celie does not leave her abusive situations earlier; and, I cannot help but be bothered by this. It seems that the students see Celie as completely trapped, while they view Melinda as having outlets to obtain help. The faulty logic that since Melinda can at any point reach out to an adult and be heard is frustrating because even her own parents disparage her obvious self-mutilation. But, I think, too, that the decades of abuse that Celie experiences is very difficult for some students to even imagine. And,

139

this difficulty in 'imagining' attests to the lack of practice in witnessing, as well as the difficulty of expressing trauma.

In the end, my students struggle with the act of witnessing with both *Speak* and *The Color Purple*. And I believe the reasons for their difficulties are largely based on the very constructions that help silence the protagonists: namely race and age. Whereas my students react with a combination of silences and ambiguous reactions, critics and mass audiences have reacted the same way. I believe that the ultimate reasons for these disparate reactions are because of Americans have become accustomed to envisioning representative black bodies in pain—while they unconsciously refuse to acknowledge representations of a child's body in severe pain. In *African Americans and the Culture of Pain*, Debra Walker King argues that "representations of the black body as torn and shamefully abused…emphasize that body's use as a metaphorical figure of pain's timeless memory" (6). In her autobiography, Angelou responds to romantic representations of Southern African-American sharecroppers:

> In later years I was to confront the stereotyped picture of gay song-singing cotton pickers with such inordinate rage that I was told even by fellow Blacks that my paranoia was embarrassing. But I had seen the fingers cut by the mean little cotton bolls, and I had witnessed the backs and shoulders and arms and legs resisting any further demands. (8)

And Celie's body, as Berlant argues, "has taken a beating, [and] it also carries the traces of her violently inscribed history" (852)—from her childhood to adulthood. hooks observes, "Slave narratives often emphasize time and time again that black people's survival was often

140

determined by their capacity to repress feelings" (*Sisters* 99). *The Color Purple* resists the need to be silent as well as the stigma of being silent, transforming silence as a form of resistance—because it is for the purpose of survival and healing.

But, I am not convinced that the representation of black bodies in is the sole reason that my students react the way that they do. The representative child's body, however, is—generally—white, middle-class, "innocent", and in need of protection; like Orphan Annie, we—as viewers—are trained to want to protect her, nurture her. Neither Celie nor Melinda is comparable to Orphan Annie; Celie's racial difference exit, but something else is missing from both Celie and Melinda's demeanor—the overly performative joy in tribulation. A bit too perky, Annie sings, "The sun'll come out tomorrow" and infuses the entire presidential suite and millionaire adopted father with optimism. Both Celie and Melinda bear witness to the ambiguous experiences and reactions of living with trauma; they do not tap dance, but they also do not get to live with Oliver "Daddy" Warbucks. And, that is the crux: socioeconomic class affects the living experiences of Celie and Melinda, as well as the cultural expectations surrounding their representations. And, maybe these are the reasons why my students (who are mainly middle-class, though from different races) feel like it is easier to talk about Melinda's experiences than Celie's; and I early await their responses this semester when I ask them my questions. I am thankful, though, for texts like *The Color Purple* and *Speak* because they not only promote witnessing within the discourse of trauma, but they also help to foster a counter-public within the classroom—and though we go our separate ways, we do so with renewed faith in community and the power of our own confessional voice.

For the tenth anniversary of *Speak*'s publication, Anderson wrote her first poem. The first and last stanzas were written by her; but, the remainder of the poem is taken from the letters that she received from fans of the novel. Formatted like a script, much like how Melinda's silences are presented as blank spaces or sparse words, the poem illustrates the variety of reactions from readers. Some confess that they are survivors of rape, others that they were not raped but are victims of domestic abuse and cut to reduce the inner pain; and, even one writer, a cheerleader, says that she sat with "that girl" at lunch after reading *Speak*. The power of the novel cannot be denied; Anderson has created multiple online discussion spaces for this counter-public that is fostered by the novel. Fans and survivors upload videos, confessing to this witnessing public—and trying to help it expand. After reading *Speak*, my students invariably inform me that the novel helped them understand the pain of those they knew who were raped and those who were bullied for being 'different' during their formative years. I'm always surprised at how shy they are in sharing with me this important information; and I'm always a bit saddened by their countenance as they speak with me. I'm sure they have much more to say; but, like Melinda, they're just beginning to speak about things they either dismissed or found too painful to discuss. And, then, I look around the room and try to find the one or two students who reminded me of Celie at the beginning of the novel: head bowed down, eyes averted, and searching. And I look forward to those moments when we all talk together—whether in confessions or silent witnessing.

Notes:

[1] Sadly, Grealy died from a heroin overdose in 2002 at the age of 39. Her short piece "Mirrors" appears in *Autobiography of a Face* and has been anthologized in several collections.

[2] See, specifically Trites 8-10.

[3] Trites credits Joseph Kett's *Rites of Passage: Adolescence in America, 1790 to the Present* (New York: Basic, 1997) with these ideas.

[4] The rhetoric of adolescence within "identity politics" is discussed in Chapter 2—specifically in relation to Medovio's theories.

[5] This act of silencing is so closely integrated with her rape that it could be considered an additional primary wound, along with the physical and sexual abuses.

[6] See Chapter 1 for a discussion about the differences between Rowson's *Charlotte Temple* and Hannah Webster Foster's *The Coquette*.

Chapter 5: (Afterward) Manifesto for a Witnessing Public

As evident in the last chapter (especially in relation to *The Color Purple*), the act of witnessing is not always easy—and it is not always without ambiguities. The texts that have been explored in the previous chapters provide readers what witnessing "looks like"—and "does not look like." Becoming familiar with the attributes and responsibilities of witnessing helps the act to become more familiar, less foreign, and therefore more apt to not frighten potential witnesses. The purpose of witnessing shifts the purpose of confession away from perpetuating a system of power and knowledge and toward the identity and agency of individual survivors. The refusal to witness begets more violence and more traumas. Resistance toward witnessing does not have to be extremely overt; it manifests itself through unwillingness to listen to others' confessions and also expectations placed upon those confessions. In this final afterward, I want to outline potential methods we—as individuals and teachers—can use in our daily lives and classrooms to promote the act of witnessing.

Types of Witnesses

Writers exist as both confessors and witnesses. hooks makes a distinction between recovery and writing: "However, writing is not therapy. Unlike therapy, where anything may be spoken in any manner, the very notion of craft suggests that the writer must necessarily edit, shape, and play with words in a manner that is always subordinated to desired intent and effect" (*Rapture* 14). Thus, writers have an agenda; they want readers to "see" something in particular. That "message" varies from text to text; for

144

instance, the tradition of American women's confessional writing that has been discussed in the previous chapters encourages witnessing. Readers' main purposes are to witness; after witnessing, though, they may become confessors. Witnessing does encourage more witnessing; this is not to suggest that confessions are simply an "incitement to discourse"—or perpetuation of language—but that the witnesses see an opportunity to take advantage of a "safe space." Within fictional texts, protagonists have the option of witnessing or wounding (because even passive listening is hurtful to the confessor) the confessor. Within in memoirs, of course, the same is possible—except that the other individuals are based on the likeness of one actual person. (Oftentimes a fictional protagonist is based on a conglomerate of actual living persons; other times, an individual in a memoir is portrayed with "liberties." This is particularly why witnessing should concentrate on the "meaning" of the written confession and be as concerned about "accuracy.") I think it is impossible to try to create a hierarchy of the power of witnessing between these groups; doing so would be like ranking types of traumas—insulting at best. What ultimately matters is validating the confessor and altering the circumstances and beliefs that help to perpetuate trauma.

Rules for Witnessing

Rule I: Just say 'No' to Confession-on-Command and Raiding 'the Closet'

Day-time talk shows have given us the false pretense that a survivor of trauma—such as survivors of rape—can be "cured" in sometimes a five- or ten-minute segment. This "cure" seems to be mostly signified by a reunion of the survivor and a friend, who becomes representative of the empathetic audience. While I believe that these talk shows have great potential, which I will address later, they create unrealistic expectations about confessing trauma. Neither experiences of trauma or confessions of trauma are single events; there is no way to encapsulate the everyday life of a survivor or their process of self-awareness. Realizing this helps witnesses as well as survivors; transforming confession as a process and performance removes the burden and strictness associated with the act of confession. Cvetkovich writes about this complicated process that survivors must undergo in order to reclaim both confession and silence:

> Indeed, many narratives by survivors of incest and sexual abuse indicate that the trauma resides as much in secrecy as in the sexual abuse—the burden not to tell creates its own network of psychic wounds that far exceed the even itself. By the same token, the work of breaking the silence about sexual abuse, like that of coming out, has to be understood as an ongoing process and performance, not as a punctual event. (94)

So, expecting someone to be completely "reborn" or transformed within less than an hour is an unhealthy fantasy to perpetuate. Guests on talk shows have their confessions, to some degree, already scripted by the show; and they are expected to compartmentalize their suffering into almost one sentence. Patience, then, is imperative—and so is not focusing on the end result, or expecting miraculous healing after confessions. Focusing on witnessing, not on the gratification, of hearing another's confession of trauma is the goal. Many talk show hosts, these days, do mention (to the guests, conveniently as the show is being filmed) that guests will have opportunities for further mental health counseling. To me, this is vital: neither survivors nor witnesses need to believe that healing is a linear process, that confession alone is the "talking cure."

Believing in the ruse that confession can forever erase the pain of trauma and survivor's guilt helps fuel the incessant desire to prompt—and often force—confessions. In relation to sexuality and sexual abuse, especially, remaining "silent" or "in the closet" is as shameful as "the secret" that is being 'hidden.' This misconception is quite dangerous and illogical. So, instead of feeling liberated by leaving "the closet" in the process of personal evolution, many people are thrust out of it "for their own good" (often by seemingly well-intentioned individuals). But, confession-on-command is not healthy, and neither is forcing someone "out of the closet." Cvetkovich writes:

> Recent queer/gay and lesbian theory, fortified by a critique of the repressive hypothesis, has been alert to the intricacies of acts of disclosure, where shifts in context, audience, and speaker can dramatically alter the meaning and effect of coming out, as well as what constitutes speaking or being silent (or silenced). (94)

Being forced "out" can be as traumatic as why the person is "in the closet" to begin with. While I do not believe that confession automatically liberates, I also do not believe that it automatically strips someone of her or his agency. Scarry posits that, while coerced confessions are a part of torture, they are not in themselves torturous. Scarry argues,

> World, self, and voice are lost, or nearly lost, through the intense pain of torture and not through the confession as is wrongly suggested by its connotations of betrayal. The prisoner's confession merely

objectifies the fact of their being almost lost, makes their invisible absence, or nearly absence, visible to the torturers. (35)

Rule II: Search for Meanings, Not Necessarily "Truth", Or Why Aliens are *Real*

Pain destroys language and defies usual documentation, so why do we persist in thinking that it will be revealed in clear, clean scientific discourse? In *Undoing Gender*, Judith Butler describes the difference between "meaning" and "truths"; she writes:

> Indeed, it may be that finding meanings is very different from finding truths, and that one way to get to meanings is to suspend the kinds of judgments that might block communication. The confession strikes me as an important moment to consider because not only does it constitute, within the psychoanalytic setting, a communication of what one's desire or deed has been, but the very speaking constitutes another act, one that within the field of the analytic setting confers a certain reality on the deed, if it is a deed in question, and that also implicates the analyst as listener in the scene of desire. (165)

If the goal is to validate the confessor's agency and to witness pain, one need not worry about interrogating the speaker—or proving her/him "wrong." Accuracy, or creating a medical chart, is not the goal—knowledge that Susanna Kaysen explicitly confronts the readers with in *Girl, Interrupted*. In fact, the ineffable—such as supernatural occurrences—are apt in describing trauma. To explain the unexplainable, confessors use the tools that are available; for instance, Mary Rowlandson uses scriptures as a tool to mark her silence and the silencing aspects of trauma. In "Telling It

Slant: The Testimony of Mercy Short," Janice Knight analyzes demonic possession as a rhetoric, within Early American culture, to articulate trauma; Knight argues that Short, whose family was killed in Indian raids and who suffered as a low-class servant, uses the diagnosis of demonic possession as "interpretive conventions and healing practices necessary to solace, and perhaps even to cure" (40). The magnitude of her pain, finally witnessed by the general Puritan society, provided Short with comfort; and, being "possessed" also serves as a way for her to "ease her survivor's guilt" (58) though suffering.

While modern narratives of trauma do not often include demonic possession, confessions of alien abductions appear as apt ways to explain the ineffable. *Mysterious Skin*, directed by Gregg Araki, focuses on two boys who were raped by their pedophilic baseball coach: one of the boys is tortured by his memories of the abuse and constantly risks his health and safety by having unprotected sex with men for money; the other cannot remember the past and believes that his inability to remember stems from being abducted by aliens. Curiously, Melinda (in *Speak*) also considers the possibility of being abducted by aliens: "I just thought of a great theory that explains everything. When I went that party, I was abducted by aliens. They have created a fake Earth and a fake high school to study me and my reactions" (Anderson 42). Melinda's attempt to rationalize what happened to her, the lack of justice, and others' cruel responses leads her to find supernatural explanations for her experiences. Does that mean that everyone in my class, when we read *Speak*, should believe in the existence of extra-terrestrial life forms? No, of course not—but we must interrogate why the rhetoric is important, why there is resistance to supernatural rhetoric as a means to articulate trauma. Aliens are 'elsewhere', apart from this earth—just like the experiences of trauma; and, abductees are powerless to stop the abduction or "experiments" that are conducted. Aliens steal, too—they steal time, memories, and even give only false or painful memories. In *Mysterious Skin*, the boy who believes that he was abducted looks at a cow with a fellow-believer, who remarks:

> Feel that? It's the sex organs. They're gone. The aliens, they experiment on cattle, because the poor things are so defenseless. Us, on the other hand—they can't kill us. They just leave behind the hidden memories of what they've done. Which in a way is almost worse. Notice anything else strange? There's no blood. They took that, too.

Only because humans are more resilient than cows are they able to survive alien abductions, the character reasons. Otherwise, the aliens would take their abductees very life.

Rule III: What Doesn't Kill Us _Can_ Kill Us

The "flip-side" of the coin is, of course, that trauma bestows some kind of eternal spring of strength. Just because someone miraculously does not die from drinking poison does not mean that person is immune to poison and should begin chugging every chemical under the kitchen sink. No, that person is still *human*, still an individual with limits and strengths. The first time that I taught *Speak*, one of my students remarked: "Well, it's like that old saying—'what doesn't kill you, makes you stronger.'" Of course, this student looked pleased, having thought of this age-old myth. Yes, it is a myth. Everyone has different "breaking points"—what I might not can "handle," one of my students may easily endure, and vice versa. That day, I was perplexed and worried about my students not taking the novel "seriously" since it is considered YA literature; but, I never expected one of them to insinuate that Melinda's rape "makes her stronger." I provided my students with a brief synopsis of Ellie Wiesel's *Night* and then asked them, "Would you say, 'Well, Ellie, it didn't kill you, man—it just made you stronger'?" They were quiet for a while, and so was I. It seems blasphemous to say something like that to someone who survived the Holocaust concentration camps, but what gives us the impression that we can use that trite phrase to anyone who has suffered any trauma? After that class, years ago, I still have this conversation with students and am anxious to hear what they think; for myself, I believe that the phrase is simply a prop—something to say after someone has shared a confession of trauma. Unable to say anything else, our impulse is to "make light" of the situation—and, that, certainly does not constitute witnessing.

When trauma survivors are still residing in abusive environments, they can very well feel like they may die—and, wretchedly, some do. Their agenda is to survive, but often through numbness; afraid, they seem passive while they are struggling with an invisible internal war. While I am not advocating pity or the martyrdom of survivors, I cannot help but feel revolted by the "simple" advice of many talk-show hosts give women who are living with their abusers. Countless reality talk shows portray a battered woman who sits on a stage, crying or emotionally numb, as the host instructs her to simply leave—as if nothing so sensible had ever crossed the battered woman's mind. The "get-over-it" and "pull-yourself-up-by-your-own-bootstraps" rhetoric ignores the intricacies of psychological states and physical captivity that are often enforced by economics and violence in situations of domestic violence toward women. I irretrievably think to myself, "Yeah, that host can say he (or she) would do so-and-so on stage, but would that change if he (or she) was placed in the house with that monster for a couple of months?" Of course, perpetrators are not tattooed "M" for monster; their ability to appear perfectly normal is part of their lure. The appearance of normality, coupled with sporadic expressions of kindness, is one of the attributes that helps a captor to maintain control over a domestic captive.

Rule IV: Witnessing is Difficult *Real* Work, or Pain is *not* Popcorn

In her discussion about the modern memoir, Nancy Miller argues that readers are almost always willing to be at least empathic toward memoirists: "autobiographers need readers—particularly to share their loss. That invitation is what makes the reader want to take the autobiographer up on the pact" (545). Embracing positionality as a witness includes empathy and sympathy, but not for ultimate reason of *taking* more from the confessor. The confessor's job is not to make you, as a witness, comfortable. Embrace being uncomfortable: it's not about you; *it's about "them."* As a witness, you have the responsibility to listen and witness. Afterwards, you may muse over what was said—and think about it in abstract ways. But remember to be pragmatic when you are creating those scenarios in your head; remember that for every representative body in your head, millions exist in the flesh. And, if you're not uncomfortable listening to someone's confession of trauma or with the prospect of so much responsibility, you might want to ask yourself, "Why?" If you find yourself becoming lackadaisical and "rolling your eyes," ask yourself why you are not taking so-and-so "seriously."

Just like the "job" of witnessing is about finding meaning and validating the confessor, it is *not* about analyzing confessions for inaccuracies. The confessor is not "on the stand" to answer your questions. In the film *Transamerica*, Bree Osbourne (played by the 'Desperate Housewife' Felicity Huffman) reunites with a son whom she never knew existed; but, the son does not know that Bree is a male-to-female transsexual. After finding out that Bree is his 'biological father', the son accuses Bree of deception. Bree responds, "Just because a person doesn't go around blabbing her entire biological history to everyone she meets doesn't make her a liar." Witnesses cannot erase the pain of trauma, but they need not cause further pain by doubting (and further wounding) the confessor.

Trashy TV can be good for you—seriously, or at least as long as you interrogate the rhetoric and your reactions, and this may annoy your fellow viewers. But no longer can it be "mindless entertainment." When Maury Povich asks the age-old question, "Is it a Boy *or* a Girl?!", you (as a witness) will have the responsibility to question many ideas, including why some audience members have so much glee pointing and laughing while human beings try to perform their genders and identities upon the stage. Memoirs, interviews, every written and oral confession: they exist to be witnessed, not for your entertainment, alone. Witnessing becomes a pedagogical event, in a way, when you ask yourself these questions: What can you learn and what does confessor want you to learn by listening.

Rule V: Create a Safe Space

This may seem common-sense, but safety is important. This "safe space" can be created in a multitude of ways, in various environments. Between two individuals, often one person makes it known that what is said must remain "in confidence." Within an intimate and trusted friend, this space is easy to achieve; however, among those who are strangers—or who have known each other for only a couple of months, it is quite a feat. But creating a safe space within a class seems to happen, on different levels, depending on the chemistry and size of the group.

As the facilitator of discussion, I create "ground-rules" that I place on the syllabus and explain to the students on the first few days of class. And, then, I even give them a graded quiz on these requirements. Institutions have various rules, forbidding sexual harassment and racial discrimination—notably. But, I make it clear to my students that any harassment or disrespect is unacceptable. Moreover, I explain to them that we, as a group, are going to strive toward *appreciating* differences—rather than simply tolerating them. Toleration is a passive stance while appreciation requires engagement, investigation, and a degree of understanding (especially ideas that are foreign).

At the end of each class, especially those that focus on the topic of confession, my students "close" the class with their own creative projects. During these presentations and final musings on the class, I generally become a bit 'misty-eyed'. Without fail, a student will share some painful piece of their experiences, or experiences that they offer up to be witnessed because they know that we (as a group) will appreciate and validate them. Several students "come out of the closet", confess being queer; some students confess physical impairments that we would never have known otherwise, like being told that they would be deaf by the age of twenty-two (and that they are now twenty-one). These confessions of trauma are not simply pieces of information; rather, the confession do not even begin to convey the difficult experiences that lead up to that moment, the internal turmoil that confession begets, the fear of rejection or further wounding, or the painful experiences are likely to follow outside of the classroom.

Teacher to Teacher

The Color Purple begins with a quote from Stevie Wonder's song "Do Like You," a song about a boy who becomes the person "who could really boogy best" because of his talent and continual desire to learn from other dancers. As any teacher knows, as time goes along, we develop our own pedagogical niche—in a way much we rarefy our personal sense of selves. I cannot honestly say how much my ability to foster a witnessing space is based on talent, luck, practice, and personality traits. I can say, though, that when I am striving to be the most conscientious witness that I can be, my students seem to have an easier time sharing, discussing, and interrogating their own ideas.

In a class full of witnesses, do not expect everyone to sing "Kumbaya" or for your job to be easy; witnessing is an intense act and certainly not static—for the students or the teacher. Since witnessing is designed to dismantle unequal distribution of power and to validate the agency of confessors, no one is "head of the class." Or, are they? I admire hooks for promoting "a democratic setting where everyone feels a responsibility to contribute" (*Teaching* 39). Like her, I try to create a setting that *appears* democratic: I sit in a circle with my students, witness their confessions and share my own, and communicate in a very accessible manner and language. But, I believe that a classroom cannot be truly "democratic." While I am conscious of the performativity of teaching, I am aware that my students sit in "circles" because I (as their teacher) ask them to. I envision the power structure in the classroom to be like the United States government: students elect to take my class, put their faith in me as a representative and mediator between them and the institution. But, I have allegiance to both the power structure—they do pay my bills (or, at least, mostly)—and the students. My point is that as teachers, we cannot delude ourselves into believing that we can destroy the grading system or writing expectations of our students' next course by choosing to sit among them versus standing behind a podium.

Although I believe that teaching is performative, I am not arguing that it is a spectacle—or making light of the political implications of radical teaching, like creating a witnessing classroom. Teaching resistance and critical consciousness is dangerous, as some departments are very much aware. Joe Marshall Hardin's *Opening Spaces: Critical Pedagogy and Resistance Theory in Composition* discusses teaching political consciousness and empowering students as a teacher's (especially an English teacher's) missions. But, this radical positionality, for a teacher, "may be professionally dangerous for composition scholars and teachers" (Hardin

51). Like hooks and other critics and teachers, Hardin advocates teaching students "to resist the uncritical acceptance of cultural representations and institutional practices by interrogating rhetoric to uncover its motives and values; and...[to teach students] to produce text that uses rhetoric and convention to give voice to their own values and positions" (7).

In *Teaching to Transgress: Education as the Practice of Freedom*, bell hooks shares her experiences and strategy for what she terms "engaged" or "transgressive" pedagogy. She argues that the main difference between this type of pedagogy and "conventional critical or feminist pedagogy" is that "it emphasizes well-being. This means that teachers must be actively committed to a process of self-actualization that promotes their own well-being if they are to teach in a manner that empowers students" (15). As a teacher, I'm sure you are quite relieved to hear that you may consider your own well-being; but, do not become too comfortable.

Your students will often confess beliefs and experiences that you find uncomfortable and too orthodox for your own liberal tastes. You already know this. But, not here's the next part: do not cringe when you hear them espouse their parents' very Republican views. Resisting that knee-jerk reaction has been one of my own personal difficulties; and, particular subjects, namely religion, are harder than others to brace myself for. While we are responsible for promoting a certain environment as teachers, we are not solely responsible for anyone except ourselves. Acknowledging our own "herstory" or "history", as it may be, is critical; we are teachers, but we are individuals first. We must never grow so tired that we forget to encourage our own personal healing and to critically interrogate our own beliefs.

One final note: as academic critics, we often look for what is lacking, what is potentially fallible. Some critics build their reputation on deconstructing and attacking others' arguments. And, while ideas and reputations should be interrogated, there comes a point to where we need to ask ourselves, "What can we take from the discussion and put into action?" As bell hooks so concisely writes, "Critique in and of itself does not lead to change" (*Feminism* 35). As students and teachers, we spend several hours in the classroom or preparing for our discussions in the classroom. That space—although political and important—is not the place where we live the bulk of our lives. Discussions and witnessing are important, but so are our actions outside that "bubble." hooks also writes, "To be truly visionary we have to root our imagination in our concrete reality while simultaneously imagining possibilities beyond that reality" (*Feminism* 100). So, in other words, we must use both our critical consciousness and imagination simultaneously in order to create viable courses of social action on the micro and macro levels.

List of References

Abbandonato, Linda. "A View from 'Elsewhere': Subversive Sexuality and
    the Rewriting of the Heroine's Story in *The Color Purple*." *PMLA*
    106.5 (Oct. 1991): 1106-1115.

Allen, Marriette Pathy. "The Making of 'Southern Comfort.'" *Transgender
    Tapestry* 103 (Fall 2003): 37-9.

Anderson, Laurie Halse. *Speak*. New York: Penguin, 1999.

---. Interview. *Speak*. New York: Penguin, 1999. 199-202.

---"Listen." *Laurie Halse Anderson's Official Web Site*. 2 February 2009
    <http://www.writerlady.com/images/SpeakPOEMinvite.gif>

Angelou, Maya. *I Know Why The Caged Bird Sings*. New York: A Bantam
    Book, 1969.

American Library Association. "Banned and/or Challenged Books from the
    Radcliffe Publishing Course Top 100 Novels of the 20th Century."
    Retrieved on January 26, 2009 from
    <http://www.ala.org/ala/aboutala/offices/oif/bannedbooksweek/bbwlin
    ks/reasonsbanned.Cfm>.

-----. "Laurie Halse Anderson wins 2009 Edwards Award for significant and
lasting

contribution to young adult readers for Catalyst; Fever 1793; and
Speak." Retrieved on January 26, 2009 from
<http://www.ala.org/ala/aboutala/offices/oif/bannedbooksweek/bbwlin
ks/reasonsbanned.cfm>.

Barnes, Elizabeth. *States of Sympathy: Seduction and Democracy in the
American Novel.* NewYork, NY: Columbia UP, 1997.

Baronin von Curtius. "Reflections of the Christine Jorgensen Case." *One
Magazine* 3.3 (March 1955): 27-28.

Beam, Alex. *Gracefully Insane: Life and Death inside American's Premier
Mental Hospital.* Cambridge: PublicAffairs, 2001.

Bebo, Jacqueline. "Sifting Through the Controversy: Reading *The Color
Purple.*" *Callaloo* 39 (Spring 1989): 332-342.

Becker, Dana. *Through the Looking Glass: Women and Borderline
Personality Disorder.* Boulder: Westview Press, 1997.

Benjamin, Harry. *The Transsexual Phenomenon.* New York: Ace
Publishing Corp., 1966.

---. "Transsexualism and Transvestism as Psycho-Somatic and Somato-
Psychic Syndromes." *The Transgender Studies Reader.* Ed. Susan
Stryker. New York: Routledge, 2006. 45-52.

Berlant, Lauren. "Race, Gender, and Nation in *The Color Purple*." *Critical Inquiry* 14 Summer 1988): 831-859.

Blakeslee, Alton. "GI-Turned-Girl Spotlights Duel Sex Nature of Thousands." *The Washington Post* 7 December 1952: M1. ProQuest Historical Newspapers. U of Florida Lib., Gainesville, FL. 1 Oct. 2006.

Bradstreet, Anne. *The Works of Anne Bradstreet.* Lennox: HardPress, 2007.

Brooks, Peter. *Troubling Confessions: Speaking Guilt in Law and Literature.* Chicago: U of Chicago P, 2000.

Brown, William Hill. *The Power of Sympathy.* New York: Penguin, 1996.

Butler, Judith. *Undoing Gender.* New York: Routledge, 2004.

Califia, Patrick. *Sex Changes: Transgender Politics.* 2nd Ed. San Francisco: Cleis Press, 2003.

Castaiglia, Christopher. *Bound and Determined: Captivity, Culture Crossing, and White Womanhood from Mary Rowlandson to Patty Hearst.* Chicago: U of Chicago P, 1996.

Castaiglia, Chris and Julia Stern. "Introduction" *Early American Literature* 36. 1 (2002): 1-7.

"Christine Back in U.S. Wearing Mink." *The Washington Post* 13 February
1953: 16. ProQuest Historical Newspapers. U of Florida Lib.,
Gainesville, FL. 1 Oct. 2006.

"Christine's Doctors Tell of Operations." *The Washington Post* 29 May
1953: 9. ProQuest Historical Newspapers. U of Florida Lib.,
Gainesville, FL. 1 Oct. 2006.

Cola, Lola. "Live Chat Interview." *BBC Four.* 19 November 2005.
<http://www.bbc.co.uk/bbcfour/documentaries/storyville/lola_chat.sht
ml>.

Colapinto, John. *As Nature Made Him: The Boy who was Raised as a Girl.*
New York: Perennial, 2001.

The Color Purple. Dir. Stephen Spielberg. Perfs. Danny Glover, Whoopi
Goldberg. DVD. Warner-Columbia Film, 1985.

Cushman, Phillip. *Constructing the Self, Constructing America: A Cultural
History of Psychotherapy.* Reading: Addison-Wesley Publishing Co.,
Inc., 1995.

Cutter, Martha J. "Philomela Speaks: Alice Walker's Revisioning of Rape
Archetypes in *The Color Purple.*" *MELUS* 24. 3/4 (Fall/Winter 2000),
pp. 161-180.

Cvetkovich, Ann. *An Archive of Feelings: Trauma, Sexuality, and Lesbian Public Cultures.* London: Duke UP, 2003.

Davidson, Cathy. *Revolution and the Word: The Rise of the Novel in Early America.* New York: Oxford UP, 1986.

Davidson, Cathy N. and Jessamyn Hatcher. Introduction. *No More Separate Spheres! A Next Wave American Studies Reader.* Durham: Duke UP, 2002. 7-26.

D'Emilio, John and Estelle B. Freedman. *Intimate Matters: A History of Sexuality in America.* 2nd ed. Chicago: U of Chicago P, 1997.

"Denmark Intends to Ban Americans in Search of Sex Operations." *The Washington Post* 6 May 1954: 62. ProQuest Historical Newspapers. U of Florida Lib., Gainesville, FL. 1 Oct. 2006.

Derounian, Kathryn Zabelle. Introduction. *Women's Indian Captivity Narratives.* New York: Penguin Books, 1998. xi-xxviii; 55-7.

-----. "The Publication, Promotion, and Distribution of Mary Rowlandson's Indian Captivity Narrative in the Seventeenth Century." *Early American Literature* 23. 3 (1988): 239-261.

Dill, Elizabeth. "A Mob of Lusty Villagers: Operations of Domestic Desires in Hannah Webster Foster's *The Coquette*." *Eighteenth-Century Fiction* 15: 2 (2003). 255-279.

Dillon, Elizabeth Maddock. *The Gender of Freedom: Fictions of Liberalism and the LiteraryPublic Sphere.* Stanford: Stanford UP, 2004.

Douglas, Ann. *The Feminization of American Culture.* New York: Farrar, Straus, & Giroux, 1998.

East of Eden. Dir. Elia Kazan. Perfs. Julia Harris, James Dean. DVD. Warner Bros., Pictures, 1955.

Elderidge, Larry D. "Crazy Brained: Mental Illness in Colonial America." *Bulletin of the History of Medicine* 70. 3 (Fall 1996): 361-386.

Evans, Gareth. "Rakes, Coquettes and Republican Patriarchs: Class, Gender and Nation in Early American Sentimental Fiction." *Canadian Review of American Studies/Canadienne d'Etudes* 35. 3 (1995): 41-61.

Fitchtelberg, Joseph. "Lovers and Citizens." *Critical Fictions: Sentiment and the American Market, 1780-1870.* Athens: U of Georgia P, 2003. 72-110.

Foucault, Michel. *The History of Sexuality: An Introduction, Volume 1.* New York: Vintage Books, 1990.

Foster, Hannah Webster. *The Coquette.* Oxford: Oxford UP, 1986.

Freud, Sigmund. *Dora: An Analysis of a Case of Hysteria*. New York: Touchstone, 1963.

Gilmore, Leigh. *The Limits of Autobiography: Trauma and Testimony*. Ithica: Cornell UP, 2001.

Girl, Interrupted. Dir. James Mangold. Perfs. Winona Ryder, Angelina Jolie. DVD. Columbia Pictures, 1999.

Grealy, Lucy. *Autobiography of a Face*. Boston: Harper Perennial, 1994.

Gregory, Elizabeth. "Confessing the Body: Plath, Sexton, Berryman, Lowell, and Ginsberg, and the gendered poetics of the 'real.'" *Modern Confessional Writing*. Ed. Jo Gill. New York: Routledge, 2006. 33-49.

Halberstam, Judith. *In a Queer Time and Place: Transgender Bodies, Subcultural Lives*. New York: New York UP, 2005.

Hall, G. Stanley. *Adolescence: Its Psychology and its Relations to Physiology, Anthropology, Sociology, Sex, Crime, Religion, and Education*. New York: D. Appleton and Company, 1907.

Hardin, Joe Marshall. *Opening Spaces: Critical Pedagogy and Resistance Theory in Composition*. New York: State U of New York P, 2001.

Hawthorne, Nathaniel. *The Scarlett Letter*. New York: Penguin Books,

2009.

Hausman, Bernice L. "Body, Technology, and Gender in Transsexual
    Autobiographies." *The Transgender Studies Reader*. Ed. Susan
    Stryker. New York: Routledge, 2006. 335-361.

Hearst, Patricia Campbell. *Every Secret Thing*. With Alvin Moscow.
    Garden City: Doubleday, 1982.

Herman, Judith. *Trauma and Recovery: The Aftermath of Violence—from
    Domestic Abuse to Political Terror*. New York: Basic Books, 1997,

hooks, bell. *Feminism is for Everybody: Passionate Politics*. Cambridge:
    South End Press, 2000.

---. *Remembered Rapture: The Writer at Work*. New York: Henry Holt and
    Company, 1999.

---. *Sisters of the Yam: black women and self-recovery*. Cambridge: South
    End Press, 2005.

---. *Talking Back: Thinking Feminist, Thinking Black*. Boston: South End
    Press, 1989.

---. *Teaching to Transgress: Education as the Practice of Freedom*. New
    York: Routledge, 1994.

Jacobs, Harriet Ann. *Incidents in the Life of a Slave Girl. The Literature of the American South.* Ed. William L. Andrews et. al. New York: W.W. Norton & Co., Inc., 1998.

Jorgensen, Christine. *A Personal Autobiography.* San Francisco: Cleis Press, 2000.

---. Interview. *Christine Jorgensen Reveals.* Interview prepared and conducted by M.R. Russell. J Records, New York. 26 Nov. 1957.

Kaplan, Amy. "Manifest Domesticity." *No More Separate Spheres! A Next Wave American Studies Reader.* Ed. Cathy N. Davidson and Jessamyn Hatcher. Durham: Duke UP, 2002. 183-207

King, Debra Walker. *African Americans and the Culture of Pain.* Charlottesville: U of Virginia P, 2008.

Knight, Janice. "Telling It Slant: The Testimony of Mercy Short." *Early American Literature* 36.1 (2002): 39-69.

Lepore, Jill. *The Name of War: King Philip's War and the Origins of American Identity.* New York: Vintage Books, 1999.

Latham, Don. "Melinda's Closet: Trauma and the Queer Subtext of Laurie Halse Anderson and *Speak.*" *Children's Literature Association Quarterly* 31.4 (Winter 2006): 369-82.

Lewis, Minday. *Life Inside: A Memoir*. New York: Atria Books, 2002.

Logan, Lisa. "Mary Rowlandson's Captivity and the 'Place' of the Woman Subject." *Early American Literature* 28.3 (1993): 255-277.

Matthiessen, F.O. *American Renaissance: Art and Expression in the Age of Emerson and Whitman*. Oxford: Oxford UP, 1941.

McClintock, Anne. "Paranoid Empire: Specters from Guantanamo and Abu Ghraib." *small axe* 26 (March 2009): 50-74.

McGee, Chris. "Why Won't Melinda Just Talk about What Happened? Speak and the Confessional Voice." *Children's Literature Association Quarterly* 34.2 (Summer 2009): 172-187.

Medovoi, Leerom. *Rebels: Youth and the Cold War Origins of Identity*. Durham: Duke UP, 2005.

Meyerowitz, Joanne. *How Sex Changed: A History of Transsexuality in the United States*. Cambridge: Harvard UP, 2002.

Miller, Nancy K. "The Entangled Self: Genre bondage in the Age of the Memoir." *PMLA* 122.2 (2007): 537-548.

Morris, Jan. *Conundrum*. New York: New York Review Books, 2002.

Mysterious Skin. Dir. Gregg Araki. Perfs. Joseph Gordon-Levitt, Chase

Ellison. DVD. Desperate Pictures, 2005.

Nadel, Alan. "Rhetoric, Sanity, and the Cold War: the Significance of
    Holden Caulfield's Testimony." *Containment Culture: American
    Narratives, Postmodernism, and the Atomic Age.* Durham: Duke UP,
    1995.

"Parents Join Ex-GI, Now a Daughter." *The Washington Post* 21 Dec.
    1952: M3. ProQuest Historical Newspapers. U of Florida Lib.,
    Gainesville, FL. 1 Oct. 2006.

Pettengill, Claire C. "Sisterhood in a Separate Sphere: Female Friendship
    in Hannah Foster's *The Coquette* and *The Boarding School.*" *Early
    American Literature* (1992): 185-203.

Prosser, Jay. *Second Skins: The Body Narratives of Transsexuality.* New
    York: Columbia UP, 1998.

Proudfit, Charles L. "Celie's Search for Identity: A Psychoanalytic
    Developmental Reading of Alice Walker's *The Color Purple.*"
    Contemporary Literature 32: 1 (Spring 1991): 12-37.

Rich, Adrienne. *Blood, Bread, and Poetry: Selected Prose, 1979-1985.*
    New York: W.W. Norton & Company, 1986.

Richardson, Samuel. *Clarissa.* Boston: Houghton Mifflin Company, 1962.

Robinson, Cynthia Cole. "The Evolution of Alice Walker." *Women's Studies* 38.3 (2009): 293-311.

Rogers, Richard. "I Enjoy Being a Girl." *Flower Drum Song: 1958 Original Broadway Cast Recording.* Perf. Pat Suzuki. Dir. Gene Kelly. Sony, 1958. CD.

Rowlandson, Mary. "The Captivity and Restoration of Mrs. Mary Rowlandson." *Journeys in New Worlds: Early American Women's Narratives.* Ed. William Andrews et al. Madison: U of Wisconsin P, 1990.

Rowson, Susanna. *Charlotte Temple.* New York: Penguin, 1991.

Rust, Marion. "What's Wrong with Charlotte Temple." *William and Mary Quarterly* 40: 2 (Jan 2003): 99-118.

Sanchs, Andrea. "The Unconfessional Confessionalist." *Time* 11 July 1994. Web. 2006. <http://www.time.com/time/magazine/article/0,9171,981084-2,00.html>.

Scarry, Elaine. *The Body in Pain: The Making and Unmaking of the World.* Oxford: Oxford UP, 1985.

Schilb, John. "Autobiography after Prozac." *Rhetorical Bodies.* Ed. Jack Selzer and Shawn Crowley. Madison: U of Wisconsin P, 1999. 202-

217.

"Second Ex-GI Becomes 'Woman' in Denmark; First Surgery on Kitchen Table at Midnight." *The Washington Post* 25 Feb. 1954: 3. ProQuest Historical Newspapers. U of Florida Lib., Gainesville, FL. 1 Oct. 2006.

Sedgwick, Catherine Maria. *Hope Leslie; or Early Times in the Massachusetts*. New Brunswick: Rutgers UP, 1984.

Sedgwick, Eve Kosofsky. *Epistemology of the Closet*. Berkley: U of California P, 1990.

-----. *Tendencies*. Durham: Duke UP, 1993.

Serlin, David. "Christine Jorgensen and the Cold War Closet." *Radical History Review* 62 (1995): 136-165.

Shneidman, Edwin S. The Suicidal Mind. New York: Oxford UP, 1996.

Showalter, Elaine. *A Jury of Her Peers: American Women Writers, from Anne Bradstreet to Annie Proulx*. New York: Alfred A. Knopf, 2009.

Southern Comfort. Dir. Kate Davis. Perfs. Robert Eads, Lola Cola. DVD. New Video Group, 2001.

Spade, Dean. "Mutilating Gender." *The Transgender Studies Reader*. Ed.

Susan Stryker. New York: Routledge, 2006. 315-332.

Speak. Dir. Jessica Sharzer. Perfs. Kristen Stewart, Michael Angarano. DVD. Showtime Networks, 2004.

Tennenhouse, Leonard. "Libertine America." *differences: A Journal of Feminist Cultural Studies* 11. 3 (1999/2000): 1-28.

Tompkins, Jane. *Sensational Designs: The Cultural Work of American Fiction 1790-1860*. New York: Oxford UP, 1985.

Traister, Bryce. "Mary Rowlandson and the Invention of the Secular." *Early American Literature* 42.2 (2007): 323-354.

Transamerica. Dir. Duncan Tucker. Perfs. Felicity Huffman, Andrea James. DVD. Belladonna Productions, 2005.

Trites, Roberta Seelinger. *Disturbing the Universe: Power and Repression in Adolescent Literature*. Iowa City: U of Iowa P, 2000.

Walker, Alice. *The Color Purple*. Orlando: Harcourt, 1982.

---. *In Search of Our Mother's Gardens*. San Diego: A Harvest/HBJ Book, 1983.

Warner, Michael. *Publics and Counter Publics*. New York: Zone Books, 2002.

---, ed. *Fear of a Queer Planet: Queer Politics and Social Theory.* Minneapolis: U of Minnesota P, 1993.

Wilchins, Riki Anne. *Queer Theory, Gender Theory: An Instant Primer.* Los Angeles: Alyson Books, 2004.

---. *Read My Lips: Sexual Subversion and the End of Gender.* Ithaca: Firebrand Books, 1997.

Whitaker, Robert. *Mad in America: Bad Science, Bad Medicine, and the Enduring Mistreatment of the Mentally Ill.* Cambridge: Perseus Publishing, 2002.

Wiesel, Elie. *Night.* Trans. Stella Rodway. New York: Bantam Books, 1960.

Wilson, Elizabeth. "Tell it like it is: Women and Confessional Writing." *Sweet Dreams: Sexuality, Gender, and Popular Fiction.* Ed. Susannah Radstone. London: Lawrence & Wishart, 1988. 21-45.

Wonder, Stevie. "Do Like You." *Hotter than July.* Motown, 1980. CD.

Wood, Mary Elene. *The Writing on the Wall: Women's Autobiography and the Asylum.* Chicago: U of Illinois P, 1994.

Wurtzel, Elizabeth. *Prozac Nation: A Memoir.* New York: Riverhead Book,

1995.

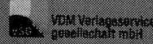

42731029R00103

Made in the USA
Lexington, KY
03 July 2015